Data Push Apps with HTML5 SSE

Darren Cook

Beijing · Cambridge · Farnham · Köln · Sebastopol · Tokyo

Data Push Apps with HTML5 SSE

by Darren Cook

Printed in the United States of America.

Published by O'Reilly Media, Inc., 1005 Gravenstein Highway North, Sebastopol, CA 95472.

O'Reilly books may be purchased for educational, business, or sales promotional use. Online editions are also available for most titles (*http://my.safaribooksonline.com*). For more information, contact our corporate/institutional sales department: 800-998-9938 or *corporate@oreilly.com*.

Editors: Simon St. Laurent and Allyson MacDonald	**Indexer:** Lucie Haskins
Production Editor: Kristen Brown	**Cover Designer:** Karen Montgomery
Copyeditor: Kim Cofer	**Interior Designer:** David Futato
Proofreader: Charles Roumeliotis	**Illustrator:** Rebecca Demarest

March 2014:   First Edition

Revision History for the First Edition:

2014-03-17:   First release

See *http://oreilly.com/catalog/errata.csp?isbn=9781449371937* for release details.

ISBN: 978-1-449-37193-7

[LSI]

Table of Contents

Preface

The modern Web is a demanding place. You have to look good. You have to load fast. And you have to have good, relevant, interesting, up-to-date content. This book is about a technology to help with the second and third of those: making sure people using your website or web application are getting content that is bang up-to-date. Minimal latency, no compromises.

This is also a book that cares about practical, real-world applications. Sure, Chapter 2 is based around a toy example, as are the introductory examples in Chapters 6 and 7. But the rest of the book is based around complete applications that don't shy away from the prickly echidnas that occupy the corner cases the real world will throw at us.

The Kind of Person You Need to Be

You need to be strong yet polite, passionate yet objective, and nice to children, the elderly, and Internet cats alike. However, this book is less demanding than real life. I'm going to assume you know your HTML (HyperText Markup Language) from your HTTP (HyperText Transport Protocol), and that you also know the difference between HTML, CSS (Cascading Style Sheets), and JavaScript. To understand the client-side code you should at least be able to read and understand basic JavaScript. (When more complex JavaScript is used, it will be explained in a sidebar or appendix.)

On the server side, the book has been kept as language-neutral as possible. Most code is introduced with simple PHP code, because PHP is quite short and expressive for this kind of application. As long as you know any C-like language you will have no trouble following along, but if you get stuck, please see Appendix C, which introduces some aspects of the PHP language. Chapter 2 also shows the example in Node.js. In later chapters, if the code gets a bit PHP-specific, I also show you how to do it in some other languages.

Finally, to follow along with the examples it is assumed you have a web server such as Apache installed on your development machine. On many Linux systems it is already there, or very simple to install. For instance, on Ubuntu, `sudo apt-get install lamp-server` will install Apache, PHP, and MySQL in one easy step. On Windows, XAMPP (*http://www.apachefriends.org/en/xampp-windows.html*) is a similar all-in-one package that will give you everything you need. There is also a Mac version (*http://www.apache friends.org/en/xampp-macosx.html*).

Organization of This Book

The core elements of SSE are not that complex: Chapter 2 shows a fully working example (both frontend and backend) in just a few pages. Before that, Chapter 1 will give some background on HTML5, data push, potential applications, and alternative technologies.

From Chapter 3 through Chapter 7 we build a complete application, trying to be as realistic as possible while also trying really hard not to bore you with irrelevant detail. The domain of this application is financial data. Chapter 3 is the core application. Chapter 4 refactors and expands on it. Chapter 5 deals with the awkward details that turn up when we try to make a data push application, things like complex data, data sources going quiet, and sockets dying on us. Chapter 6 introduces one way (long-polling) to get our application working on desktop and mobile browsers that are not yet supporting SSE, and then Chapter 7 shows two other ways that are superior but not available on all browsers. Chapter 3 also spends some time developing realistic, repeatable data that our sample application can push. Though not directly about SSE, it is a very useful demonstration of designing for testability in data push applications.

Chapter 8 covers some elements of the SSE protocol that we chose not to use in the realistic application that was built up in the other chapters. And, yes, the reasons why they were not used is also given. That leads into Chapter 9, where all the security issues (cookies, authorization, CORS) that were glossed over in earlier chapters are finally covered.

Conventions Used in This Book

The following typographical conventions are used in this book:

Italic
> Indicates new terms, URLs, email addresses, filenames, and file extensions.

`Constant width`
> Used for program listings, as well as within paragraphs to refer to program elements such as variable or function names, databases, data types, environment variables, statements, and keywords.

`Constant width bold`
> Shows commands or other text that should be typed literally by the user.

Constant width italic

> Shows text that should be replaced with user-supplied values or by values determined by context.

 This element signifies a tip or suggestion.

 This element signifies a general note.

 This element indicates a warning or caution.

Using Code Examples

The source files used and referred to in the book are available for download at *https://github.com/DarrenCook/ssebook*.

This book is here to help you get your job done. In general, if example code is offered with this book, you may use it in your programs and documentation. You do not need to contact us for permission unless you're reproducing a significant portion of the code. For example, writing a program that uses several chunks of code from this book does not require permission. Selling or distributing a CD-ROM of examples from O'Reilly books does require permission. Answering a question by citing this book and quoting example code does not require permission. Incorporating a significant amount of example code from this book into your product's documentation does require permission.

We appreciate, but do not require, attribution. An attribution usually includes the title, author, publisher, and ISBN. For example: "*Data Push Apps with HTML5 SSE* by Darren Cook (O'Reilly). Copyright 2014 Darren Cook, 978-1-449-37193-7."

If you feel your use of code examples falls outside fair use or the permission given above, feel free to contact us at *permissions@oreilly.com*.

Safari® Books Online

 Safari Books Online (*www.safaribooksonline.com*) is an on-demand digital library that delivers expert content in both book and video form from the world's leading authors in technology and business.

Technology professionals, software developers, web designers, and business and creative professionals use Safari Books Online as their primary resource for research, problem solving, learning, and certification training.

Safari Books Online offers a range of product mixes and pricing programs for organizations, government agencies, and individuals. Subscribers have access to thousands of books, training videos, and prepublication manuscripts in one fully searchable database from publishers like O'Reilly Media, Prentice Hall Professional, Addison-Wesley Professional, Microsoft Press, Sams, Que, Peachpit Press, Focal Press, Cisco Press, John Wiley & Sons, Syngress, Morgan Kaufmann, IBM Redbooks, Packt, Adobe Press, FT Press, Apress, Manning, New Riders, McGraw-Hill, Jones & Bartlett, Course Technology, and dozens more. For more information about Safari Books Online, please visit us online.

How to Contact Us

Please address comments and questions concerning this book to the publisher:

O'Reilly Media, Inc.
1005 Gravenstein Highway North
Sebastopol, CA 95472
800-998-9938 (in the United States or Canada)
707-829-0515 (international or local)
707-829-0104 (fax)

We have a web page for this book, where we list errata, examples, and any additional information. You can access this page at *http://oreil.ly/data-push-apps-html5-sse*.

To comment or ask technical questions about this book, send email to *bookquestions@oreilly.com*.

For more information about our books, courses, conferences, and news, see our website at *http://www.oreilly.com*.

Find us on Facebook: *http://facebook.com/oreilly*

Follow us on Twitter: *http://twitter.com/oreillymedia*

Watch us on YouTube: *http://www.youtube.com/oreillymedia*

CHAPTER 1

All About SSE...And Then Some

SSE stands for *Server-Sent Events* and it is an *HTML5 technology* to allow the server to *push* fresh data to clients. It is a superior solution to having the client poll for new data every few seconds. At the time of writing it is supported natively by 65% of desktop and mobile browsers, but in this book I will show how to develop fallback solutions that allow us to support more than 99% of desktop and mobile users. By the way, 10 years ago I used Flash exclusively for this kind of data push; things have evolved such that nothing in this book uses Flash.

The browser percentages in this book come from the wonderful "Can I Use..." website (*http://caniuse.com/eventsource*). It, in turn, gets its numbers from StatCounter GlobalStats (*http://gs.statcounter.com/*). And, to preempt the pedants, when I say "more than 99%" I really mean "it works on every desktop or mobile browser I've been able to lay my hands on." Please forgive me if that doesn't turn out to be exactly 99% of your users.

For users with JavaScript disabled, there is no hope: neither SSE nor our clever fallback solutions will work. However, because being told "impossible" annoys me as much as it annoys you, I will show you a way to give even these users a dynamic update (see "What If JavaScript Is Disabled?" on page 93).

The rest of this chapter will describe what HTML5 and data push are, discuss some potential applications, and spend some time comparing SSE to WebSockets, and comparing both of those to not using data push at all. If you already have a rough idea what data push is, I'll understand if you want to jump ahead to the code examples in Chapter 2, and come back here later.

HTML5

I introduced SSE as an *HTML5* technology earlier. In the modern Web, HTML is used to specify the structure and content of your web page or application, CSS is used to describe how it should look, and JavaScript is used to make it dynamic and interactive.

 JavaScript is for actions, CSS is for appearance; notice that HTML is for both structure *and* content. Two things. First, the logical organization (the "DOM"); second, the data itself. Typically when the data needs to be updated, the structure does not. It is this desire to change the content, without changing the structure, that drove the creation of data pull and data push technologies.

HTML was invented by Tim Berners-Lee, in about 1990. There was never a formally released HTML 1.0 standard, but HTML 2.0 was published at the end of 1995. At that time, people talked of Internet Years as being in terms of months, because the technology was evolving very quickly. HTML 2.0 was augmented with tables, image uploads, and image maps. They became the basis of HTML 3.2, which was released in January 1997. Then by December 1997 we had HTML 4.0. Sure, there were some tweaks, and there was XHTML, but basically that is the HTML you are using today—unless you are using HTML5.

Most of what HTML5 adds is optional: you can mostly use the HTML4 you know and then pick and choose the HTML5 features you want. There are a few new elements (including direct support for video, audio, and both vector and bitmap drawing) and some new form controls, and a few things that were deprecated in HTML4 have now been removed. But of more significance for us is that there are a whole bunch of new JavaScript APIs, one of which is Server-Sent Events. For more on HTML5 generally, the Wikipedia entry (*http://en.wikipedia.org/wiki/HTML5*) is as good a place to start as any.

The orthogonality of the HTML5 additions means that although all the code in this book is HTML5 (as shown by the `<!doctype html>` first line), just about everything not directly to do with SSE will be the HTML4 you are used to; none of the new HTML5 tags are used.

Data Push

Server-Sent Events (SSE) is an HTML5 technology that allows the server to *push fresh data* to clients (commonly called *data push*). So, just what is data push, and how does it differ from anything else you may have used? Let me answer that by first saying what it is not. There are two alternatives to data push: no-updates and data pull.

The first is the simplest of all: no-updates (shown in Figure 1-1). This is the way almost every bit of content on the Web works.

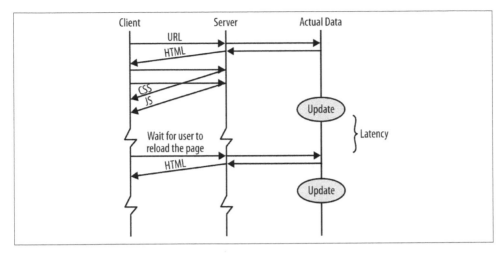

Figure 1-1. Alternative: no-updates

You type in a URL, and you get back an HTML page. The browser then requests the images, CSS files, JavaScript files, etc. Each is a static file that the browser is able to cache. Even if you are using a backend language, such as PHP, Ruby, Python, or any of the other dozens of choices to *dynamically* generate the HTML for the user, as far as the browser is concerned the HTML file it receives is no different from a handmade static HTML file. (Yes, I know you can tell the browser not to cache the content, but that is missing the point. It is still static.)

The other alternative is data pull (shown in Figure 1-2).

Based on some user action, or after a certain amount of time, or some other trigger, the browser makes a request to the server to get an up-to-date version of some, or all, of its data. In the crudest approach, either JavaScript or a meta tag (see "What If JavaScript Is Disabled?" on page 93) tells the whole HTML page to reload. For that to make sense, either the page is one of those made dynamically by a server-side language, or it is static HTML that is being regularly updated.

In more sophisticated cases, Ajax techniques are used to just request fresh data, and when the data is received a JavaScript function will use it to update part of the DOM. There is a very important concept here: only fresh data is requested, not all the structure on the HTML page. This is really what we mean by data pull: pulling in just the new data, and updating just the affected parts of our web page.

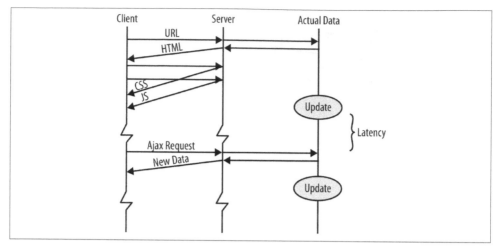

Figure 1-2. Alternative: data pull (regular polling)

Jargon alert. Ajax? DOM?

Ajax is introduced in Chapter 6, when we use it for browsers that don't have native SSE support. I won't tell you what it stands for, because it would only confuse you. After all, it doesn't have to be asynchronous, and it doesn't have to use XML. It is hard to argue with the J in Ajax, though. You definitely need JavaScript.

DOM? Document Object Model. This is the data structure that represents the current web page. If you've written `document.getE lementById('x')....` in JavaScript, or `$('#x')....` in JQuery, you've been using the DOM.

That is what data push isn't. It is not static files. And it is not a request made by the browser for the latest data. Data push is where the *server* chooses to send new data to the clients (see Figure 1-3).

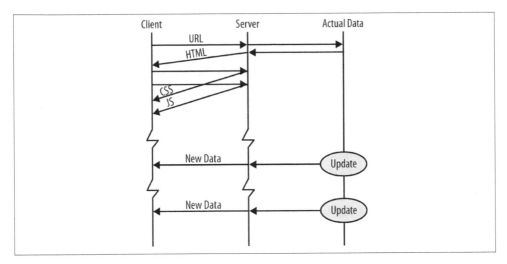

Figure 1-3. Data push

When the data source has new data, it can send it to the client(s) immediately, without having to wait for them to ask for it. This new data could be breaking news, the latest stock market prices, a chat message from another online friend, a new weather forecast, the next move in a strategy game, etc.

The *functionality* of data pull and data push is the same: the user gets to see new data. But data push has some advantages. Perhaps the biggest advantage is lower latency. Assuming a packet takes 100ms to travel between server and client, and the data pull client is polling every 10 seconds, with data push the client gets to see the data 100ms after the server has it. With data pull, the client gets to see the data between 100ms and 10100ms (average 5100ms) after the server has it; everything depends on the timing of the poll request. On average, the data pull latency is 51 times worse. If the data pull method polls every 2 seconds, the average comes down to 1100ms, which is merely 11 times worse. However, if no new data were available, that would result in more wasted requests and more wasted resources (bandwidth, CPU cycles, etc.).

That is the balancing act that will always be frustrating you with data pull: to improve latency you have to poll more often; to save bandwidth and connection overhead you have to poll less often. Which is more important to you—latency or bandwidth? When you answer "both," that is when you need a data push technology.

Other Names for Data Push

The need for data push is as old as the Web,[1] and over the years people have found many novel solutions, most of them with undesirable compromises. You may have heard of some other technologies—Comet, Ajax Push, Reverse Ajax, HTTP Streaming—and be wondering what the difference is between them. These are all talking about the same thing: the fallback techniques we will study in Chapters 6 and 7. SSE was added as an HTML5 technology to have something that is both easy to use and efficient. If your browser supports it, SSE is always[2] superior to the Comet technologies. (Later in this chapter is a discussion of how SSE and WebSockets differ.)

By the way, you will sometimes see SSE referred to as `EventSource`, because that is the name of the related object in JavaScript. I will call it SSE everywhere in this book, and I will only use `EventSource` to refer to the JavaScript object.

Potential Applications

What is SSE good for? SSE excels when you need to update part of a web application with fresh data, without requiring any action on the part of the user. The central example application we will use to explore how to implement data push and SSE is pushing foreign exchange (FX) prices. Our goal is that each time the EUR/USD (Euro versus US Dollar) exchange rate changes at our broker, the new price will appear in the browser, as close to *immediately* as physically possible.

This fits the SSE protocol perfectly: the updates are frequent and low latency is important, and they are all flowing from the server to the client (the client never needs to send prices back). Our example backend will fabricate the price data, but it should be obvious how to use it to distribute real data, FX or otherwise.

With only a drop of imagination you should be able to see how this example can apply to other domains. Pushing the latest bids in an auction web application. Pushing new reviews to a book-seller website. Pushing new high scores in an online game. Pushing new tweets or news articles for keywords you are interested in. Pushing the latest temperatures in the core of that Kickstarter-financed nuclear fusion reactor you have been building in your back garden.

Another application would be sending alerts. This might be part of a social network like Facebook, where a new message causes a pop up to appear and then fade away. Or it

---

1. If you think data push and data pull only became possible with Ajax (popularized in 2005), think again. Flash 6 was released in March 2002 and its Flash Remoting technology gave us the same thing, but with no annoying browser differences (because just about everyone had Flash installed at that time).

2. Well, okay, not always *always*. See "When Data Push Is the Wrong Choice" on page 9 and "Is Long-Polling Always Better Than Regular Polling?" on page 88.

might be part of the interface for an email service like Gmail, where it inserts a new entry in your inbox each time new mail arrives. Or it could be connected to a calendar, and give you notice of an upcoming meeting. Or it could warn you of your disk usage getting high on one of your servers. You get the idea.

What about chat applications? Chat has two parts: receiving the messages of others in the chat room (as well as other activities, such as members entering or leaving the chat room, profile changes, etc.), and then posting your messages. This two-way communication is usually a perfect match for WebSockets (which we will take a proper look at in a moment), but it does not mean it is not also a good fit for SSE. The way you handle the second part, posting your messages, is with a good old-fashioned Ajax request.

As an example of the kind of "chat" application to which SSE is well-suited, it can be used to stream in the tweets you are interested in, while a separate connection is used for you to write your own tweets. Or imagine an online game: new scores are distributed to all players by SSE, and you just need a way to send each player's new score to the server at the end of their game. Or consider a multiplayer real-time strategy game: the current board position is constantly being updated and is distributed to all players using SSE, and you use the Ajax channel when you need to send a player's move to the central server.

Comparison with WebSockets

You may have heard of another HTML5 technology called WebSockets, which can also be used to push data from server to client. How do you decide if you should be using SSE or WebSockets? The executive summary goes like this: anything you can do with WebSockets can be done with SSE, and vice versa, but each is better suited to certain tasks.

WebSockets is a more complicated technology to implement server side, but it is a real two-way socket, which means the server can push data to the client and the client can push data back to the server.

Browser support for WebSockets is roughly the same as SSE: most major desktop browsers support both.[3] The native browser for Android 4.3 and earlier supports neither, but Firefox for Android and Chrome for Android have full support. Android 4.4 supports both. Safari has had SSE support since 5.0 (since 4.0 on iOS), but has only supported WebSockets properly since Safari 6.0 (older versions supported an older version of the protocol that had security problems, so it ended up being disabled by the browsers).

---

3. Internet Explorer is the exception, with no native SSE support even as of IE11; WebSocket support was added in IE10.

SSE has a few notable advantages over WebSockets. For me the biggest of those is convenience: you don't need any new components—just carry on using whatever backend language and frameworks you are already used to. You don't need to dedicate a new virtual machine, a new IP, or a new port to it. It can be added just as easily as adding another page to an existing website. I like to think of this as the *existing infrastructure advantage*.

The second advantage is server-side simplicity. As we will see in Chapter 2, the backend code is literally just a few lines. In contrast, the WebSockets protocol is *complicated* and you would never think to tackle it without a helper library. (I did; it hurt.)

Because SSE works over the existing HTTP/HTTPS protocols, it works with existing proxy servers and existing authentication techniques; proxy servers need to be made WebSocket aware, and at the time of writing many are not (though this situation will improve). This also ties into another advantage: SSE is a text protocol and you can debug your scripts very easily. In fact, in this book we will use curl and will even run our backend scripts directly at the command line when testing and developing.

But that leads us directly into a potential advantage of WebSocket over SSE: it is a binary protocol, whereas SSE uses UTF-8. Sure, you could send binary data over the SSE connection: the only characters with special meaning in SSE are CR and LF, and those are easy to escape. But binary data is going to be *bigger* when sent over SSE. If you are sending large amounts of binary data from server to client, WebSockets is the better choice.

Binary Data Versus Binary Files

If you want to send large binary *files* over either WebSockets or SSE, stop and think if that is what you should be doing. Wouldn't using good old HTTP for that be better? It will save you from having to reinvent all kinds of wheels (authorization, encryption, proxies, caching, keep-alive). And, if your concern is efficient use of socket connections, take a good look at HTTP/2.0.[4]

When I talk about "large amounts of binary data" I mean when you need to implement binary Internet protocols, such as SSH, inside a browser. If all you want to do is push a new banner ad to a user, the best way is to send just the URL over SSE (or WebSockets), and then have the browser use good old HTTP to fetch it.

But the biggest advantage of WebSockets over SSE is that it is two-way communication. That means it is just as easy to send data *to* the server as to receive data *from* the server. When using SSE, the way we normally pass data from client to server is using a separate

---

4. See *http://en.wikipedia.org/wiki/HTTP_2.0*, or check out *High Performance Browser Networking* by Ilya Grigorik (O'Reilly).

Ajax request. Relative to WebSockets, using Ajax in this way adds overhead. However, it only adds a bit of overhead,[5] so the question becomes: when does it start to matter? If you need to pass data to the server once/second or even more frequently, you should be using WebSockets. Once every one to five seconds and you are in a gray area; it is unlikely to matter whether you go with WebSockets or SSE, but if you are expecting heavy load it is worth benchmarking. Less frequently than once every five or so seconds and you won't notice the difference.

What of performance for passing data from the server to the client? Well, assuming it is textual data, not binary (as mentioned previously), there is no difference between SSE and WebSockets. They are both are using a TCP/IP socket, and both are lightweight protocols. No difference in latency, bandwidth, or server load…except when there is. Eh? What does that mean?

The difference applies when you are enjoying the *existing infrastructure* advantage of SSE, and have a web server sitting between your client and your server script. Each SSE connection is not just using a socket, but it is also using up a thread or process in Apache. If you are using PHP, it is starting a new PHP instance especially for the connection. Apache and PHP will be using a chunk of memory, and that limits the number of simultaneous connections you can support. So, to get the exact same data push performance for SSE as you get for WebSockets, you have to write your own backend server. Of course, those of you using Node.js will be using your own web server anyway, and wonder what the fuss is about. We take a look at using Node.js to do just that, in Chapter 2.

A word on WebSocket fallbacks for older browsers. At the moment just over two-thirds of browsers can use these new technologies; on mobile it is a lower percentage. Traditionally, when a two-way socket was needed, Flash was used, and polyfill of WebSockets is often done with Flash. That is complicated enough, but when Flash is not available it is even worse. In simple terms: WebSocket fallbacks are hard, SSE fallbacks are easier.

When Data Push Is the Wrong Choice

Most of what I will talk about in this section applies equally well to both the HTML5 data push technologies (SSE and WebSockets) and the fallback solutions we will look at in Chapters 6 and 7; the thing they have in common is that they keep a dedicated socket open for each connected client.

First let us consider the static situation, with no data push involved. Each time users open a web page, a socket connection is opened between their browser and your server. Your server gathers the information to send back to them, which may be as simple as

---

5. Well, a few hundred bytes in HTTP/1.1, even more if you have lots of cookies or other headers being passed. In HTTP/2.0, it is much less.

loading a static HTML file or an image from disk, or as complex as running a server-side language that makes multiple database connections, compiles CoffeeScript to Java-Script, and combines it all together (using a server-side template) to send back. The point being that once it has sent back the requested information, the socket is then closed.[6] Each HTTP request opens one of these relatively short-lived socket connections. These sockets are a limited resource on your machine, but as each one completes its task, it gets thrown back in the pile to be recycled. It is really very eco-friendly; I'm surprised there isn't government funding for it.

Now compare that to data push. You never finish serving the request: you always have more information to send, so the socket is kept open forever. Therefore, because they are a limited resource,[7] we have a limit on the number of SSE users you can have connected at any one time.

You could think of it this way. You are offering telephone support for your latest application, and you have 10 dedicated call center staff, servicing 1,000 customers. When a customer hits a problem he calls the support number, one of the staff answers, helps him with the problem, then hangs up. At quiet times some of your 10 staff are not answering calls. At other times, all 10 are busy and new callers get put into a queue until a staff member is freed up. This matches the typical web server model.

But now imagine you have a customer call and say: "I don't have a problem at the moment, but I'm going to be using your software for the next few hours, and if I have a problem I want to get an immediate answer, and not risk being put on hold. So could you just stay on the line, please?" If you offer this service, and the customer has no questions, you've wasted 10% of your call center capacity for the duration of those few hours. If 10 customers did this, the other 990 customers are effectively shut out. This is the data push model.

But it is not always a bad thing. Consider if that user had one question every few seconds for the whole afternoon. By keeping the line open you have not wasted 10% of your call capacity, but actually increased it! If he had to make a fresh call (data pull) for each of those questions, think of the time spent answering, identifying the customer, bringing up his account, and even the time spent with a polite good-bye at the end. There is also the inefficiency involved if he gets a different staff member each time he calls, and they have to get up to speed each time. By keeping the line open you have not only made that

---

6. Most requests actually use HTTP persistent connection, which shares the socket between the first HTML request and the images; the connection is then killed after a few seconds of no activity (five seconds in Apache 2.2). I just mention this for the curious; it makes no difference to our comparison of the normal web versus data push solutions.

7. How limited? It depends on your server OS, but maybe 60,000 per IP address. But then the firewall and/or load balancer might have a say. And memory on your server is a factor, too. It makes my head hurt trying to think about it in this way, which is why I prefer to benchmark the actual system you build to find its limits.

customer happier, but also made your call center more efficient. This is data push working at its best.

The FX trading prices example, introduced earlier, suits SSE very well: there are going to be lots of price changes, and low latency is very important: a customer can only trade at the current price, not the price 60 seconds ago. On the other hand, consider the long-range weather forecast. The weather bureau might release a new forecast every 30 minutes, but most of the time it won't change from "warm and sunny." And latency is not too critical either. If we don't hear that the forecast has changed from "warm and sunny" to "warm and partly cloudy" the very moment the weather forecasters announce it, does it really matter? Is it worth holding a socket open, or would straightforward polling (data pull) of the weather service every 30 or 60 minutes be good enough?

What about infrequent events where latency *does* matter? What if we know there will be a government announcement of economic growth at 8:30 a.m. and we want it shown to customers of our web application as soon as the figures are released? In this case we would do better to set a timer that does a long-poll Ajax call (see Chapter 6) that would start just a few seconds before the announcement is due. Holding a socket open for hours or days beforehand would be a waste.

A similar situation applies to predictable downtime. Going back to our example of receiving live FX prices, there is no point holding the connection open on the weekends. The connection could be closed at 5 p.m. (New York local time) on a Friday, and a timer set to open it again at 5 p.m. on Sunday. If your computer infrastructure is built on top of a pay-as-you-go cloud, that means you can shut down some of your instances Friday evening, and therefore cut your costs by up to 28%! See "Adding Scheduled Shutdowns/Reconnects" on page 68, in Chapter 5, where we will do exactly that.

Decisions, Decisions…

The previous two sections discussed the pros and cons of data pull, SSE, and WebSockets, but how do you know which is best for you? The question is complex, based on the behavior of the application, business decisions about customer expectations for latency, business decisions about hosting costs, and the technology that customers and your developers are using. Here is a set of questions you should be asking yourself:

- How often are server-side events going to happen?

  The higher this is the better data push (whether SSE or WebSockets) will be.

- How often are client-side events going to happen?

  If such events occur less than once every five seconds, and especially if there is less than one event every second, WebSockets is going to be a better choice than SSE. If such events occur less than once every 5 to 10 seconds, this becomes a minor factor in the decision-making process.

- Are the server-side events not just fairly infrequent but also happening at predictable times?

  When such events are less frequent than once a minute, data pull has the advantage that it won't be holding open a socket. Be aware of the issues with lots of clients trying to all connect at the same time.

- How critical is latency? Put a number on it.

  Is an extra half a second going to annoy people? Is an extra 60 seconds not really going to matter?

  The more that latency matters, the more that data push is a superior choice over data pull.

- Do you need to push binary data from server to client?

  If there is a lot of binary data, WebSockets is superior to SSE. (It might be that XHR polling is better than SSE too.)

  If the binary data is small, you can encode it for use with SSE, and the difference is a matter of a few bytes.

- Do you need to push binary data from client to server?

  This makes no difference: both XMLHttpRequest[8] (i.e., Ajax, which is how SSE sends messages from client to server), and WebSockets deal with binary data.

- Are most of your users on landline or on mobile *connections*?

  Notebook users who are using an LTE WiFi router, or who are *tethering*, count as mobile users. A phone that has a strong WiFi connection to a fiber-optic upstream connection counts as a landline user. It is the connection that matters, not the power of the computer or the size of the screen.

  Be aware that mobile connections have much greater latency, especially if the connection needs to wake up. This makes data pull (polling) a worse choice on mobile connections than on landline connections.

  Also, a WiFi connection that is overloaded (e.g., in a busy coffee shop) drops more and more packets, and behaves more like a mobile connection than a landline connection.

- Is battery life a key concern for your mobile users?

  You have a compromise to make between latency and battery life. However, data pull (except the special case where the polling can be done predictably because you

---

8. Strictly, the second version of `XMLHttpRequest`. See *http://caniuse.com/xhr2*. IE9 and earlier and Android 2.x have no support. But none of those browsers support WebSockets or SSE either, so it still has no effect on the decision process.

know when the data will appear) is generally going to be a worse choice than data push (SSE or WebSockets).

- Is the data to be pushed relatively small?

Some 3G mobile connections have a special low-power mode that can be used to pass small messages (200 to 1000 bps). But that is a minor thing. More important is that a large message will be split up into TCP/IP segments. If one of those segments gets lost, it has to be resent. TCP guarantees that data arrives in the order it was sent, so this lost packet will hold up the whole message from being processed. It will also block later messages from arriving. So, on noisy connections (e.g., mobile, but also an overloaded WiFi connection), the bigger your data messages are the more extra packets that will get sent.

Consider using data push as a control channel, and telling the browser to request the large file directly. This is very likely to be processed in its own socket, and therefore will not block your data push socket (which exists because you said latency was important).

- Is the data push aspect a side feature of the web application, or the main thing? Are you short on developer resources?

SSE is easier to work with, and works with existing infrastructure, such as Apache, very neatly. This cuts down testing time. The bigger the project, and the more developer resources you have, the less this matters.

 For more technical details on some of the subjects raised in the previous few sections, and especially if efficiency and dealing with high loads are your primary concern, I highly recommend *High Performance Browser Networking*, by Ilya Grigorik (O'Reilly).

Take Me to Your Code!

In brief, if you have data on your website that you'd like to be fresher, and are currently using Ajax polling, or page reloads, or thinking about using them, or thinking about using WebSockets but it seems rather low level, then SSE is the technology you have been looking for. So without further delay, let's jump into the Hello World example of the data push world.

CHAPTER 2

Super Simple Easy SSE

This chapter will introduce a simple frontend and backend that uses SSE to stream real-time data to a browser client from a server. I won't get into some of the exotic features of SSE (those are saved for Chapters 5, 8, and 9). I also won't try to make it work on older browsers that do not support SSE (see Chapters 6 and 7 for that). But, even so, it will work on recent versions of most of the major browsers.

 Any recent version of Firefox, Chrome, Safari, iOS Safari, or Opera will work. It won't work on IE11 and earlier. It also won't work on the native browser in Android 4.3 and earlier. To test this example on your Android phone or tablet, install either Chrome for Android or Firefox for Android. Alternatively, wait for Chapter 6 where we will implement long-poll as a fallback solution. For the latest list of which browsers support SSE natively, see *http://caniuse.com/eventsource*.

If you want to go ahead and try it out, put *basic_sse.html* and *basic_sse.php* in the same directory,[1] a directory that is served by Apache (or whatever web server you use). It can be on localhost, or a remote server. If you've put it on localhost, in a directory called *sse*, then the URL you browse to will be *http://localhost/sse/basic_sse.html*. You should see a timestamp appearing once per second, and it will soon fill the screen.

Minimal Example: The Frontend

I will take this first example really slowly, in case you need an HTML5 or JavaScript refresher. First, let's create a minimal file, just the scaffolding HTML/head/body tags. The

---

1. For the moment, stick to keeping your HTML and your server-side script on the same machine. In Chapter 9 we will cover *CORS*, which (in some browsers) will allow the server-side script to be on a different machine.

very first line is the doctype for HTML5, which is much simpler than the doctypes you might have seen for HTML4. In the <head> tag I also specify the character set as UTF-8, not because I use any exotic Unicode in this example, but because some validation tools will complain if it is not specified:

```
<!doctype html>
<html>
  <head>
    <meta charset="UTF-8">
    <title>Basic SSE Example</title>
  </head>
  <body>
    <pre id="x">Initializing...</pre>
  </body>
</html>
```

You can also see I have a <pre> tag, with the id set to "x". I have used a <pre> tag rather than a <p> or <div> tag so that it can be filled with the received data (which contains line feeds) without any modification or formatting.

 Be aware of the potential for JavaScript injection when using server-side data with no checking.

Initially the <pre> block is hardcoded to say "Initializing...." We will replace that text with our data.

JQuery Versus JavaScript

In case you've been using JQuery everywhere, the equivalent of $("#x") to get a reference to x in your HTML is document.getElementById("x"). To replace the text, we assign it to innerHTML. To append to the existing text, we use += instead of = like this:

```
//Equivalent of $("#x").html("New content\n");
document.getElementById("x").innerHTML = "New content\n"
//Equivalent of $("#x").append("Append me\n");
document.getElementById("x").innerHTML += "Append me\n"
```

Now let's add a <script> block, at the bottom of the HTML body:

```
<!doctype html>
<html>
  <head>
    <meta charset="UTF-8">
    <title>Basic SSE Example</title>
  </head>
```

```
  <body>
    <pre id="x">Initializing...</pre>
    <script>
    var es=new EventSource("basic_sse.php");
    </script>
  </body>
</html>
```

We created an EventSource object that takes a single parameter: the URL to connect to. Here we connect to *basic_sse.php*. Congratulations, we now have a working SSE script. This one line is connecting to the backend server, and a steady stream of data is now being received by the browser. But if you run this example, you'd be forgiven for thinking, "Well, this is dull."

To see the data that SSE is sending us we need to handle the "message" event. SSE works asynchronously, meaning our program does not sit there waiting for the server to tell it something, and meaning we do not need to poll to see if anything new has happened. Instead our JavaScript gets on with its life, interacting with the user, making silly animations, sending key presses to government organizations, and whatever else we use JavaScript for. Then when the server has something to say, a function we have specified will be called. This function is called an "event handler"; you might also hear it referred to as a "callback." In JavaScript, objects generate events, and each object has its own set of events we might want to listen for. To assign an event handler in JavaScript, we do the following:

```
es.addEventListener('message',FUNCTION,false);
```

The es. at the start means we want to listen for an event related to the EventSource object we have just created. The first parameter is the name of the event, in this case 'message'. Then comes the function to process that event.[2]

The FUNCTION we use to process the event takes a single parameter, which by convention will be referred to simply as e, for event. That e is an object, and what we care about is e.data, which contains the new message the server has sent us. The function can be defined separately, and its name given as the second parameter. But it is more usual to use an anonymous function, to save littering our code with one-line functions (and having to think up suitable names for them). Putting all that together, we get this:

```
<!doctype html>
<html>
  <head>
    <meta charset="UTF-8">
    <title>Basic SSE Example</title>
  </head>
  <body>
```

---

2. The third parameter of false means handle the event in the bubbling phase, rather than the capturing phase. Yeah, whatever. Just use false.

```
    <pre id="x">Initializing...</pre>
    <script>
    var es = new EventSource("basic_sse.php");
    es.addEventListener("message", function(e){
      //Use e.data here
      },false);
    </script>
  </body>
</html>
```

Still it does nothing! So in the body of the event handler function, let's have it append e.data to the <pre> tag. (We prefix a line feed so each message goes on its own line.) The final frontend code looks like this:

```
<!doctype html>
<html>
  <head>
    <meta charset="UTF-8">
    <title>Basic SSE Example</title>
  </head>
  <body>
    <pre id="x">Initializing...</pre>
    <script>
    var es = new EventSource("basic_sse.php");
    es.addEventListener("message", function(e){
      document.getElementById("x").innerHTML += "\n" + e.data;
      },false);
    </script>
  </body>
</html>
```

At last! We see one line that says "Initializing…," then a new timestamp appears every second (see Figure 2-1).

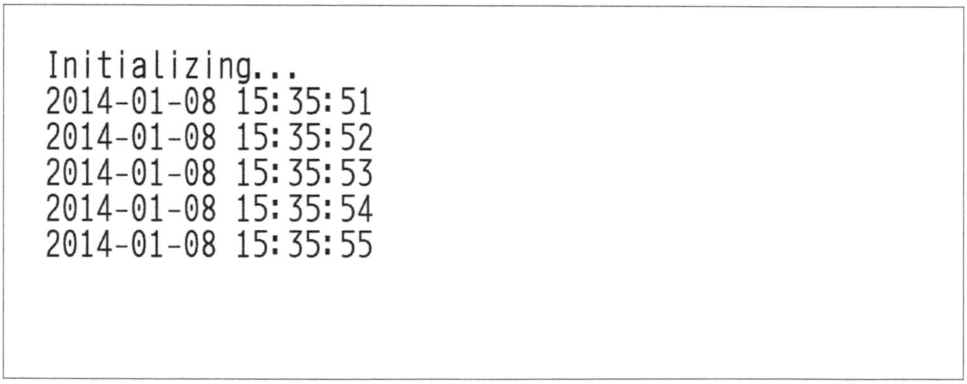

```
Initializing...
2014-01-08 15:35:51
2014-01-08 15:35:52
2014-01-08 15:35:53
2014-01-08 15:35:54
2014-01-08 15:35:55
```

Figure 2-1. basic_sse.html after running for a few seconds

We could be writing handlers for other `EventSource` events, but they are all optional, and I will introduce them later when we first need them.

Using JQuery?

Nowadays most people use jQuery. However, the SSE boilerplate code is so easy there is not much for JQuery to simplify. For reference, here is the minimal example rewritten for JQuery:

```
<!doctype html>
<html>
  <head>
    <meta charset="UTF-8">
    <title>Basic SSE Example</title>
    <script src="//code.jquery.com/jquery-1.11.0.min.js"></script>
  </head>
  <body>
    <pre id="x">Initializing...</pre>
    <script>
    var es = new EventSource("basic_sse.php");
    es.addEventListener("message", function(e){
      $("#x").append("\n" + e.data);
      },false);
    </script>
  </body>
</html>
```

This next version (*basic_sse_jquery_anim.html* in the book's source code) spruces it up with a fade-out/fade-in animation each time. This version also does a replace instead of an append, so you get to see only the most recent item:

```
<!doctype html>
<html>
  <head>
    <meta charset="UTF-8">
    <title>Basic SSE Example</title>
    <script src="//code.jquery.com/jquery-1.11.0.min.js"></script>
  </head>
  <body>
    <pre id="x">Initializing...</pre>
    <script>
    var es = new EventSource("basic_sse.php");
    es.addEventListener("message", function(e){
      $("#x").fadeOut("fast", function(){
        $("#x").html(e.data);
        $("#x").fadeIn("slow");
        });
      },false);
    </script>
  </body>
</html>
```

Minimal Example: The Backend

The first backend (server-side) example we will study is written in PHP, and looks like this:

```php
<?php
header("Content-Type: text/event-stream");
while(true){
  echo "data:".date("Y-m-d H:i:s")."\n\n";
  @ob_flush();@flush();
  sleep(1);
  }
```

Just like the frontend code, this is wonderfully short, isn't it? No libraries, no dependencies, just a few simple lines of vanilla PHP. And just like the frontend there is more we could be doing, but again it is all optional.

Going through the script, the very first line, `<?php`, identifies this as a PHP script. Then we send back a MIME type of `text/event-stream`, using the `header()` function. `text/event-stream` is the special MIME type for SSE. Next we enter an infinite loop (`while(true){...}` is the PHP idiom for that), and in that loop we output the current timestamp every second.

The SSE protocol just involves prefixing our message data (the timestamp) with `data:` and following it with a blank line. So starting at 1 p.m. on February 28, 2014, it outputs:

```
data:2014-02-28 13:00:00

data:2014-02-28 13:00:01

data:2014-02-28 13:00:02

data:2014-02-28 13:00:03

...
```

What about the `@ob_flush;@flush();` line? This tells PHP (and Apache) to send the data back to the client immediately, rather than buffer it up and send it back in batches. The `@` prefix means suppress errors, and is fine here: there are no interesting errors we need to know about, but `ob_flush()` might complain if there is no data to flush out. (In case you wondered, the order does matter. `ob_flush()` must come before `flush()`.)

PHP Error Suppression

For the PHP experts: @ is said to be slow. But putting that in context, it adds on the order of 0.01ms to call it twice, as shown here. So, as long as you are not putting it inside a tight loop, just relax. `@foo()` is shorthand for `$prev=error_reporting(0);` before the call to `foo()`, then `error_reporting($prev);` afterwards. So if you are really performance-sensitive and you find a need to use `@foo()` in a loop, and understand the implications, it is better to put those commands outside the loop.

In the case of `ob_flush`, it is an `E_NOTICE` that we want to suppress. So this an even better longhand:

```
$prev = error_reporting();
error_reporting($prev & ~E_NOTICE);
...
ob_flush();
flush();
...
error_reporting($prev);
```

http://bit.ly/1gCNyfX suggests `flush()` can never throw an error, so @ could be dropped there, and we can just leave it on `ob_flush()`. *http://bit.ly/1elPD1S* shows the notices PHP might throw from `ob_flush()`.

Do infinite loops make you nervous? It is OK here. We are using up one of Apache's threads/processes, but as soon as the browser closes the connection (whether from JavaScript, or the user closing the window) the socket is closed, and Apache will close down the PHP instance.

What about caching, whether by the client or intermediate proxies, you may wonder? I agree, caching would be awfully bad for SSE: the whole point is we have new information we want the user to know about. In my testing the client has never cached anything. Because this is intended as a minimal example, I chose to ignore caching. Examples in other chapters will send headers that explicitly request no caching, just to be on the safe side (see "Cache Prevention" on page 82).

 One other thing to watch out for when using SSE is that the browser might kill the connection if it goes quiet. For instance, some versions of the Chrome browser kill (and reopen) the connection after 60 seconds. In our real applications we will deal with this (see "Adding Keep-Alive" on page 60). Here it is not needed, because the backend never goes quiet—we output something every single second.

The Backend in Node.js

In this section I will use the Node.js language for the backend. Node.js is the same JavaScript you know from the browser, even with the same libraries (strings, regexes, dates, etc.), but done server side, and then extended with loads of modules. The biggest thing to watch out for when using Node.js is that, by default, everything is nonblocking —asynchronous, in other words—and asynchronous coding needs a different mindset. But it is this nonblocking, event-driven, behavior that makes it well-suited to data push applications.

The PHP server solution we used earlier is better termed "Apache+PHP" because Apache (or the web server of your choice) handles the HTTP request handling (and a whole heap of other stuff, such as authentication), and PHP just handles the logic of the request itself. Apart from keeping the code samples fairly small, this is also the most common way people use PHP. Node.js comes with its own web server library, and that is the way most people use it for serving web content—so that is the way we will use it here.

 Let's not get drawn into language wars. All languages suck until you are used to them. Then they just suck in ways you know how to deal with. The *real* strengths of PHP and Node.js are rather similar: very popular, easy to find developers for, and lots of useful extensions.

Minimal Web Server in Node.js

So, before I show how to support SSE with Node.js, we should first take a look at the minimal web server in Node.js:

```
var http = require("http");

http.createServer(function(request,response){
  response.writeHead(200,
    { "Content-Type": "text/plain" }
    );
  var content="Hello World\n";
  response.end(content);
  }).listen(1234);
```

The first line includes the http library; this is the CommonJS way of importing a module. We can then start running an HTTP server with a single line:

```
http.createServer(myRequestHandler).listen(port);
```

There is a lot of power in that single line: it will start listening on the port we give, handle all the HTTP protocol, and handle multiple clients, and when each client connects the specified request handler is called. By default it will listen on all local IP addresses. If you just wanted it to listen on 127.0.0.1, specify that as follows:

```
http.createServer(myRequestHandler).listen(port,"127.0.0.1");
```

By convention the request handler is implemented with an anonymous function, and our example follows that convention. The function takes two parameters: `request`, which is an instance of `http.ClientRequest`,[3] and `response`, which is an instance of `http.ServerResponse`.[4]

The `request` parameter tells us what the client is asking for. The `response` object is then used to give it to the client. This minimal example completely ignores the user request: everybody gets the same thing (the `content` string). We make two calls on the `response` object. The first is to specify the status (HTTP status code 200 means "Success") and content-type header (here plain text, not HTML). The second call, `response.end(content)`, is a shortcut for two calls: `response.write(content)` to send data to the client (optionally specifying the encoding), and `response.end()` to say that is everything that needs to be sent, we are done.

To test this code, save it as *basic_sse_node_server1.js*, and from the command line run `node basic_sse_node_server1.js`. Then in your browser visit *http://127.0.0.1:1234/*, and you should see "Hello World."

Pushing SSE in Node.js

In the previous section we ignored the user input, and output static plain-text content. For the next block of code we continue to ignore the user input, but output dynamic text—the current timestamp, just as our earlier PHP code did:

```
var http = require("http");

http.createServer(function(request, response){
    response.writeHead(200, { "Content-Type": "text/event-stream" });
    setInterval(function(){
        var content = "data:" +
            new Date().toISOString() + "\n\n";
        response.write(content);
    }, 1000);
}).listen(1234);
```

The first change is trivial: output the `text/event-stream` content type. But the biggest change from the previous example is the addition of `setInterval( ... ,1000)` to run some code once per second. In PHP we used an infinite loop, and a `sleep(1)` command to run a command once per second. If we did that in Node.js we would block the whole web server, and no other clients could connect. When writing a Node.js HTTP server, it is important to exit the request handler as quickly as possible. So the Node.js way is

---

3. See *http://nodejs.org/api/http.html#http_class_http_clientrequest*.

4. See *http://nodejs.org/api/http.html#http_class_http_serverresponse*.

to use `setInterval`. The code being called once each second is reasonably straightforward. The "data:" prefix and the "\n\n" suffix are the SSE protocol. `new Date().toISO String()` is the JavaScript idiom to get the current timestamp.

From the command line, start this with `node basic_sse_node_server2.js`. Don't try to test it in a browser just yet (it won't work). If you have `curl` installed, you can test with `curl http://127.0.0.1:1234/`. A new timestamp will appear once a second, with a blank line between each:

```
data:2014-02-28T13:00:00.123Z

data:2014-02-28T13:00:01.145Z

data:2014-02-28T13:00:02.140Z

data:2014-02-28T13:00:03.142Z

...
```

Some Improvements

There are a couple of ways we can enhance the script, though they get away from this chapter's theme of *minimal*. At the top, add this line:

```
var port = parseInt( process.argv[2] || 1234 );
```

Then change the final line of the script so it looks like this:

```
...
}).listen(port);
```

This allows you to specify the port to listen to, on the command line. If you do not have a web server already running, you could run the script as root specifying port 80.

The next change is to give some insight into how it is working. Replace `re sponse.write(content);` with these three lines:

```
var b = response.write(content);
if(!b)console.log("Data queued (content=" + content + ")");
else console.log("Flushed! (content=" + content + ")");
```

Just as in the browser, JavaScript `console.log()` is used to let the programmer see what is going on. The return value from `response.write()` is true if the data got flushed out cleanly. This happens most of the time, and it is good. It is false if the data had to be cached in memory first. That means that at the time `response.write()` returned, the data had not been sent to your client yet. This happens if you try to send data too quickly (this is hard to see; even changing the interval from 1000ms to 1ms won't count as "too quickly," but getting rid of `setInterval` and using a `while(true){...}` loop will do it), or if the socket has become broken.

Start the node server again, and then start your curl client again. Wait for some data to come through. Now press Ctrl-C to kill the curl client. Over in the node window see how it is still trying to send data. Uh-oh…that is something else Apache takes care of for us when we use Apache+PHP.

What we need to do is recognize when the client has disconnected, which can be done by listening for the "close" event. The "close" event is part of request.connection, so we can respond to it by adding this code:

```
request.connection.on("close", function(){
    response.end();
    clearInterval(timer);
    console.log("Client closed connection. Aborting.");
});
```

This code has to come *after* the call to setInterval. Just before that, capture the return value of setInterval as follows:

```
var timer = setInterval(function(){
    ...
```

So, now when the client disconnects, that function triggers and we get to cleanly close the response, as well as shut down the interval that was ticking away every second.

If you look at *basic_sse_node_server3.js* in the book's source code, you will also spot a couple of extra console.log() commands.

Now to Get It Working in a Browser!

First, start up your node server (node basic_sse_node_server3.js), look up *basic_sse.html* from earlier in this chapter, open it in an editor, and find this line:

```
var es = new EventSource("basic_sse.php");
```

Change it to use our Node.js server that is listening on port 1234:

```
var es = new EventSource("http://127.0.0.1:1234/");
```

Now open *basic_sse.html* in your browser. (This is assuming you have Apache listening on port 80, serving at least HTML files.)

Nothing happens. You will see "Preparing…," and it just sits there. Why? The problem is that the HTML is being loaded from port 80, but is then trying to make a connection to port 1234. A different port number is enough for it to count as a different server and that is not allowed (for security reasons). We will look at cross-origin resource sharing (CORS) in Chapter 9, which gives servers a way to say they want to accept connections from clients that loaded their content from somewhere else. But the alternative is to use Node.js to deliver the HTML file to the clients; this is the normal way to do things in the Node.js world.

(Before you go any further, change back *basic_sse.html* to connect to *basic_sse.php* again.) Then, so the script can read files from the local filesystem, add this line to the top of your script:

```
var fs = require("fs");
```

Then the big change is at the top of the request handler. Add this block:

```
if(request.url!="/basic_sse.php"){
  fs.readFile("basic_sse.html",
    function(err,file){
      response.writeHead( 200,
        {"Content-Type" : "text/html"}
        );
      response.end(file);
      });
  return;
  }
```

When you get a certain URL, treat it as a request for the streaming. But the rest of the time (notice the !=) send back the HTML file instead. `readFile()` is one of Node.js's async operations. You give the filename, then an anonymous function to deal with the content when it has been loaded. In the meantime, while waiting for the file to be loaded, you return from the request handler. When the file does load, we simply spit it out to the client, with a `text/html` content type, and `end()` the connection.

Now you can browse to *http://127.0.0.1:1234* in your browser.

Modifying the HTML File

What's that? Why do we mention "php" in the preceding code snippet? You've gone to all the trouble of those language wars with the PHP Brigade, going so far as to drug their tea, complain about their personal hygiene to the boss, and email them over 35 links to articles on how important and easy async programming really is, and now it looks like you are using Node.js to serve PHP content. The reason is simple: *basic_sse.html* was written to connect to the PHP script, and I don't want to make another file.

Well, this is easy to fix. Between loading the file from disk and sending it to the client, why not modify the URL it says to connect to! Make the following highlighted changes:

```
if(request.url != "/sse"){
  fs.readFile("basic_sse.html",
    function(err,file){
      response.writeHead( 200,
        {"Content-Type" : "text/html"}
        );
      var s = file.toString();
      s = s.replace("basic_sse.php","sse");
      response.end(s);
      });
```

```
        return;
        }
```

By the way, file is actually a buffer, not a string (because it might contain binary data), which is why we first have to convert it to a string.

You can find the final file with the code from this section and from the two sidebars in the book's source code as *basic_sse_node_server.js*, and here it is in full:

```javascript
var http = require("http"), fs = require("fs");
var port = parseInt( process.argv[2] || 1234 );

http.createServer(function(request, response){
  console.log("Client connected:" + request.url);
  if(request.url!="/sse"){
    fs.readFile("basic_sse.html", function(err,file){
      response.writeHead(200, { 'Content-Type': 'text/html' });
      var s = file.toString();  //file is a buffer
      s = s.replace("basic_sse.php","sse");
      response.end(s);
      });
    return;
    }
  //Below is to handle SSE request. It never returns.
  response.writeHead(200, { "Content-Type": "text/event-stream" });
  var timer = setInterval(function(){
    var content = "data:" + new Date().toISOString() + "\n\n";
    var b = response.write(content);
    if(!b)console.log("Data got queued in memory (content=" + content + ")");
    else console.log("Flushed! (content=" + content + ")");
    },1000);
  request.connection.on("close", function(){
    response.end();
    clearInterval(timer);
    console.log("Client closed connection. Aborting.");
    });
  }).listen(port);
console.log("Server running at http://localhost:" + port);
```

It is quite a bit more code than *basic_sse.php* because it is doing the tasks that Apache was taking care of in the Apache+PHP solution.

Smart, Sassy Exit

So that was the Hello World of the SSE world. Just a few lines on the frontend and a few lines on the backend; it couldn't be simpler, could it? In the next five chapters we build on this knowledge to make something more sophisticated and robust that is usable on practically every desktop and mobile browser.

CHAPTER 3

A Delightfully Realistic Data Push Application

This chapter will build upon the code we created in the previous chapter to implement a realistic (warts and all) data push application (see the next section for the problem domain that has been chosen). For this chapter and the following two, the code we build will still only work in browsers with SSE support; then in Chapters 6 and 7, I will show how you can adapt both the frontend and backend to work with older browsers.

 Because this chapter is SSE only, if you are testing on an Android device you need to install either Firefox for Android or Chrome for Android. If you are testing on Windows, install Firefox, Chrome, Safari, or Opera. C'mon, I'm sure you already have at least one of those installed—you told me you were a professional developer!

This chapter contains a bit of backend PHP code that may not feel relevant to your own application. I suggest you at least skim it, because you will see it built upon in later chapters and it shows, step-by-step, one approach for unit testing and functional testing of data push systems.

Our Problem Domain

The problem domain I will cover in this and the next few chapters is from the finance industry. It has its own jargon—almost as bad as the software industry—so I will introduce some of the terminology you will meet, and just enough background information to help you understand some of the design decisions.

The job of our application is to broadcast *FX bid/ask quotes* from a *bank or broker* to *traders*. The first bit of jargon is FX. This stands for Foreign eXchange; in other words, the buying and selling of currencies. It is a global *decentralized market*. Yikes, more jargon. A decentralized market means there is no single place where currencies are traded. Compare this to a stock exchange, where there is a single place to buy and sell shares in a company. (That is not strictly true; large companies might list their shares on two or three stock exchanges.)

The broker is a business. But it doesn't try to make money off of speculating about currency movements the way the traders do. Instead, brokers make their money off of the spread (and sometimes a commission as well). The spread is the difference between the bid and the ask price. The bid price is the lower of the two prices: it is how much the broker is willing to buy the currency for. It is how much you get if you choose to sell. The ask price is slightly higher and is how much the broker is willing to sell for. It is how much you have to pay if you want to buy.

The FX market is global. The New York stock market is just open during business hours in the New York time zone. But people want to buy and sell currencies all throughout the day, all around the world. It is a 24/5 market. By convention it opens at 5 p.m. on Sunday, New York local time (which is the start of the business week in New Zealand), and closes at 5 p.m. on Friday, again New York time.

The major currencies that are traded, with their abbreviations, are US dollar (USD), the euro (EUR), Japanese yen (JPY), British pound (GBP), Australian dollar (AUD), Canadian dollar (CAD), and the Swiss franc (CHF). Typically, an FX broker will be listing between 6 and 40 FX pairs (also called *symbols*).

What does all this mean to us?

- We have to send two prices from the server to the client, along with a timestamp.
- We need to do this for more than one currency pair.
- We have to do it with minimal latency (sudden movements and stale prices will cost our traders money).
- Our application will be running for 120 hours in a row, then will have nothing to do for 48 hours, before the cycle repeats.

The Backend

The backend demonstrated in this chapter is more complicated than the one shown in Chapter 2. We want multiple data feeds (aka symbols); call it *multiplexing* when you need to impress your boss. We want it to be used for repeatable tests, we want realistic-looking data, and we want it to be in sync for each client that connects. All without using a database. Those are quite a few demands! But it can be done. We will use a few techniques:

- Use a one-line JSON protocol.

- Use a random seed. A given random seed will always give the same stream of data. In our case it will give a completely predictable set of ticks for each symbol.
- Allow the random seed to be specified by the client. This allows a client to request the same test data over and over.
- Add together cycles of different periods, with a bit of random noise added on. This makes the data look realistic. (This book is not the place for a discussion of random walks and efficient market theory. Find a passing economist if you are interested in that subject.)
- Measure clock drift and adjust for it.

Design for Testability

There are two ways to design any system, with regard to testing. The first is with no consideration for testability. The second is to make it easy to test; but this does not usually come for free, because it often requires adding extra variables and extra functions.

However, a system that has been designed for testability is not just easier to test, it is *faster to test*. In extreme cases it can be the difference between calling a getter (completing a test in a matter of milliseconds), and a horribly complicated solution involving screen scraping and OCR that takes seconds to run. That has a knock-on effect: tests that complete quickly are run more often, bugs are found sooner and in less time, so your product is delivered sooner and is of better quality. If your test suite can be run every 5 minutes, then when it breaks, you instantly know which line of code broke it. Contrast this with a test suite that is so slow it can only be run on the weekend. You come in Monday morning and it might take you until Tuesday to work out which of your changes last week introduced the problem. (The complex testing solutions also tend to be *fragile* —sensitive to minor changes in layout, for instance.)

In our case, our system spits out random (okay, pseudorandom) data. *Design for Testability* here means taking control of the random sequence, so it can be exactly repeated if the need arises. This is a testing design pattern called *Parameter Injection*.

To complicate things, there might not just be memory and CPU involved, but also a network—so runtime could vary quite a lot from test run to test run, and we put timestamps to millisecond accuracy in the JSON we send back. Therefore, we need to find a way to make sure the timestamps are repeatable. How we tackle this is covered in the main text. (If we didn't do this, our choice would just be to range-check the fields in the data we get: make sure each timestamp is formatted correctly and is later than the previous timestamp, make sure the prices are between 95.00 and 105.00, etc. This is better than nothing, but could lead to missing subtle bugs and regressions.)

The first design decision we will make is to pass JSON strings as the message. We'll send back exactly one JSON string per line, and one per message. This is a reasonable design decision anyway, because JSON is flexible and allows hierarchical data, but as you will see in later chapters the one-line-per-message decision makes adapting our code to non-supporting browsers easier.

If you read "Our Problem Domain" on page 29 on the FX industry, you will know we are broadcasting both bid and ask quotes. I chose to do this deliberately, rather than just send a single price, because it makes things harder. If the server just has a single price we'd be tempted to make simpler design decisions. Then we would need to do lots of refactoring if we decided to add a second value. By using two pieces of data, it will be easy to change our code to support N pieces of data; and it will still work fine even if we only have a single value.

Figure 3-1 shows the high-level view of what the backend's main loop (a deliberate infinite loop, just as in Chapter 2) will be doing.

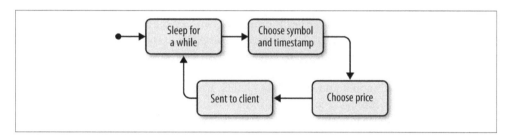

Figure 3-1. Backend's main loop

Before we enter that loop we have some initialization steps: define a class, create our test symbols, process client input parameters, and set the `Content-Type` header. Here is our first draft of the script, using hardcoded prices (where the only initialization step we need at this stage is setting the header):

```php
<?php
header("Content-Type: text/event-stream");

while(true){
  $sleepSecs = mt_rand(250,500)/1000.0;
  usleep( $sleepSecs * 1000000 );

  $d=array(
    "timestamp" => gmdate("Y-m-d H:i:s"),
    "symbol" => "EUR/USD",
    "bid" => 1.303,
```

```
    "ask" => 1.304,
    );
echo "data:".json_encode($d)."\n\n";
@ob_flush();@flush();
}
```

Rather than try to debug it over an SSE connection, I suggest you first run it from the command line:

```
php fx_server.hardcoded.php
```

That is one of the beauties of the SSE protocol: it is a simple text protocol. Press Ctrl-C to stop it. You should have seen output like this:

```
data:{"timestamp":"2014-02-28 06:09:03","symbol":"EUR\/USD","bid":1.303, ↵
    "ask":1.304}

data:{"timestamp":"2014-02-28 06:09:04","symbol":"EUR\/USD","bid":1.303, ↵
    "ask":1.304}

data:{"timestamp":"2014-02-28 06:09:08","symbol":"EUR\/USD","bid":1.303, ↵
    "ask":1.304}
```

Note that the forward slash in EUR/USD gets escaped in the JSON. Also, because of the call to gmdate those are GMT timestamps we see there. This is a good habit: always store and broadcast your data in GMT, and then adjust on the client if you want it shown in the user's local time zone.

JSON/SSE Protocol Overhead

How much wastage is there in choosing JSON for all data transmission? For instance, how does the use of JSON compare with sending our data using a minimalist CSV encoding (data:2014-02-28 03:15:24,EUR/USD,1.303,1.304). And how much wastage is there in the SSE protocol itself?

The last question is easy: the SSE overhead is 6 bytes per message, the "data:" and the extra line break. This is compared to the fallback approaches we will look at in Chapters 6 and 7.

Our JSON string is longer than it needs to be; to make it readable I have chosen verbose names, but the JSON message could instead have looked like this:

```
data:{"t":"2014-02-28 06:09:03","s":"EUR\/USD","b":1.303,"a":1.304}
```

What about a binary protocol? Well, neither JavaScript nor SSE get on well with binary, but ignoring that, let's have 4 bytes for the timestamp (though if you need milliseconds, or want it to work past 2030, you will end up using 8 bytes), 7 bytes plus a zero-terminator for the symbol, and 8 bytes each for bid/ask as doubles. That gives us 28 bytes (assuming end-of-record is implicit). Table 3-1 summarizes all that.

Because we flush data immediately (to get minimal latency), you might want to also include the overhead of a TCP/IP packet and Ethernet frame around each message. That might be fair if you are comparing to a polling approach. For instance, if the pushed data averages one message per second, there will be 59 times more TCP/IP packets compared to a once-every-60-second-poll. Possibly even more if WiFi and mobile networks are involved. But if polling (and especially if long-polling, see Chapter 6), don't forget to allow for the HTTP headers, in each direction, on each request. Remember cookies and auth headers get sent with every request, too.

As I mentioned in Chapter 1, if you want to make a useful comparison of two alternatives, in my opinion the best way is to build both approaches, and then benchmark each, under the most realistic load you can manage. Unless you are building an intranet application, *realistic* also means the server and the test clients should be in different data centers.

Table 3-1. Byte comparison of different data formats

	Using SSE	Using Fallbacks
Binary	34	28
CSV	46	40
JSON-short	69	63
JSON-readable	86	80

Before you make decisions based on those numbers though, remember that SSE communication can, and should, be gzipped, and you can expect that the more compact your format, the less compression gzip can do.

Our FX data will be nice and regular, so you might be tempted to go with CSV instead of JSON. I am going to continue to use JSON because in other applications your data might not be so simple (JSON can cope with nested data structures) and because it makes development easier if we need to add another field. In fact, you will see a more complicated data structure being used as this application evolves. And I will stick with readable field names, to help us keep our sanity.

Our first draft, *fx_server.hardcoded.php*, implements two of the three parts of our high-level algorithm: it sleeps and it sends the data to the client. In the next section we will implement choosing the symbol and price instead of hardcoding them.

The Frontend

We are going to develop the backend a lot more, but now that we have the simplest possible server-side script, let's create the simplest possible HTML page to go with it:

```
<!doctype html>
<html>
  <head>
  <meta charset="UTF-8">
  <title>FX Client: latest prices</title>
  </head>
  <body>

    <table border="1" cellpadding="4" cellspacing="0">
     <tr><th>USD/JPY</th><th>EUR/USD</th><th>AUD/GBP</th></tr>
     <tr><td id="USD/JPY"></td><td id="EUR/USD"></td><td id="AUD/GBP"></td></tr>
    </table>

    <script>
    var es = new EventSource("fx_server.hardcoded.php");
    es.addEventListener("message", function(e){
      var d = JSON.parse(e.data);
      document.getElementById(d.symbol).innerHTML = d.bid;
      },false);
    </script>

  </body>
</html>
```

When you load that in a browser you will see a three-cell table, and the middle cell, labelled EUR/USD, will appear as 1.303. Then nothing. It looks as dull as dishwater, doesn't it? But, behind the scenes, the server is actually sending the 1.303 over and over again. This frontend, basic though it is, will work with each of the improvements we are about to make to the backend.

If you followed along in Chapter 2, the first two lines of the JavaScript should look familiar. Create an EventSource object, specifying the server to connect to. Then assign a message event handler. e.data contains a string in JSON format, so the first line of our event handler is var d=JSON.parse(e.data);[1] to turn that into a JavaScript object.

 If the JSON data is bad, it will throw an exception. Starting in Chapter 5, we will wrap it in try and catch, as part of making the code production quality.

---

1. Every browser that supports SSE has JSON.parse. However, when we talk about fallbacks for older browsers we will find JSON.parse is not available in really old browsers, most notably IE6/IE7. There is a simple way to patch it, though.

The other line of our event handler starts with `document.getElementById(d.sym bol)`, which finds the HTML table cell that has been marked with one of `id="USD/ JPY"`, `id="EUR/USD"`, and `id="AUD/GBP"`.[2] Then the second half of that line fills it with the bid price: `.innerHTML=d.bid;`.

We will come back and do more on the frontend, but now let's go back and work on the backend some more.

Realistic, Repeatable, Random Data

Earlier we created a script that does repeatable data; now we have to make it random and realistic. The first problem with *fx_server.hardcoded.php* is that there is only a single symbol (currency pair); I want different symbols. Because each symbol has a lot in common and only the numbers will be different, I have created a class, `FXPair`, as shown in the following code. If PHP classes look unfamiliar, see "Classes in PHP" on page 197 in Appendix C.

```php
<?php
class FXPair{
  /** The name of the FX pair */
  private $symbol;
  /** The mean bid price */
  private $bid;
  /** The spread. Add to $bid to get "ask" */
  private $spread;
  /** Accuracy to quote prices to */
  private $decimalPlaces;
  /** Number of seconds for one bigger cycle */
  private $longCycle;
  /** Number of seconds for the small cycle */
  private $shortCycle;

  /** Constructor */
  public function __construct($symbol,$b,$s,$d,$c1,$c2){
    $this->symbol = $symbol;
    $this->bid = $b;
    $this->spread = $s;
    $this->decimalPlaces = $d;
    $this->longCycle = $c1;
    $this->shortCycle = $c2;
  }
```

---

2. DOM IDs in HTML5 can contain just about anything except whitespace. However, if you need this code to run on HTML4 browsers such as IE7 or IE8, you will need to sanitize the symbol names that the data feeds gives you. For example, convert all nonalphanumerics to "_", and make the DOM IDs "USD_JPY", "EUR_USD", etc. (Also make sure a digit is not the first character, and for IE6 (!!) support, make sure an underline is also not the first character.)

```php
/** @param int $t Seconds since 1970 */
public function generate($t){
$bid = $this->bid;
$bid+= $this->spread * 100 *
  sin( (360 / $this->longCycle) * (deg2rad($t % $this->longCycle)) );
$bid+= $this->spread * 30 *
  sin( (360 / $this->shortCycle) *(deg2rad($t % $this->shortCycle)) );
$bid += (mt_rand(-1000,1000)/1000.0) * 10 * $this->spread;
$ask = $bid + $this->spread;

return array(
  "timestamp"=>gmdate("Y-m-d H:i:s",$t),
  "symbol"=>$this->symbol,
  "bid"=>number_format($bid,$this->decimalPlaces),
  "ask"=>number_format($ask,$this->decimalPlaces),
  );
}

}
```

We have member values for bid, spread, and decimal places. For our purposes, bid stores the mean price: our values will fluctuate around this price. spread is the difference between the bid and ask prices (see "Our Problem Domain" on page 29). Why do we have a value to store the number of decimal places? By convention, currencies involving JPY (Japanese yen) are shown to three decimal places; others are shown to five decimal places.

We then have two more member variables: long_cycle and short_cycle. If you look at generate you will see these control the speed at which the price rises and falls. We use two cycles to make the cyclical behavior more interesting; the first, slower cycle has a weight of 100, and the second, shorter cycle has a relative weight of 30. In addition, we add in some random noise, with a weight of 10. Are you wondering about (mt_rand(-1000,1000)/1000.0)? PHP does not have a function for generating random floating point numbers. So we create a random integer between –1000 and +1000 (inclusive) and then divide by 1000 to turn it into a –1.000 to +1.000 random float. In each case, we multiply by the spread and by the weight.

See "Random Functions" on page 198 in Appendix C for why we use mt_rand, and how the random seed is set.

Finally, generate returns an associative array (aka an object in JavaScript, a dictionary in .NET, a map in C++) of the values. We use number_format to chop off extra decimal places. So, 98.1234545984 gets turned into 98.123.

Now how do we use this class? At the top of *fx_server.seconds.php* we create one object for each FX pair (EUR/USD appears twice because we want it to update twice as often):

```php
$symbols = array(
  new FXPair("EUR/USD", 1.3030, 0.0001, 5, 360, 47),
  new FXPair("EUR/USD", 1.3030, 0.0001, 5, 360, 47),
  new FXPair("USD/JPY", 95.10, 0.01, 3, 341, 55),
  new FXPair("AUD/GBP", 1.455, 0.0002, 5, 319, 39),
  );
```

Next, in our main loop we choose which symbol to modify randomly:

```php
$ix = mt_rand(0,count($symbols)-1);
```

And then the hardcoded $d array in *fx_server.hardcoded.php* can be replaced with a call to generate:

```php
$d = $symbols[$ix]->generate($t);
```

The full *fx_server.seconds.php* is shown here:

```php
<?php
include_once("fxpair.seconds.php");

header("Content-Type: text/event-stream");

$symbols = array(
  new FXPair("EUR/USD", 1.3030, 0.0001, 5, 360, 47),
  new FXPair("EUR/USD", 1.3030, 0.0001, 5, 360, 47),
  new FXPair("USD/JPY", 95.10, 0.01, 3, 341, 55),
  new FXPair("AUD/GBP", 1.455, 0.0002, 5, 319, 39),
  );

while(true){
  $sleepSecs = mt_rand(250,500)/1000.0;
  usleep( $sleepSecs * 1000000 );

  $t = time();
  $ix = mt_rand(0,count($symbols)-1);
  $d = $symbols[$ix]->generate($t);
  echo "data:".json_encode($d)."\n\n";
  @ob_flush();@flush();
  }
```

Note a few things about this code. The price we generate is solely based on the current time. We never store a previous value, which we then increase/decrease randomly; this might have been your first idea for implementing random prices. As well as being nice and clean and enabling repeatable, reliable testing, this also brings with it a little bonus: we can put two entries for EUR/USD in our array to get twice as many prices generated for it.

See "Falling Asleep" on page 200 in Appendix C for why I use usleep() instead of sleep().

Do you wonder why we assign $t in the main loop, when all we do is pass it to gener
ate()? Why not put the $t = time(); inside of generate()? This comes back to Design
for Testability: by using a parameter we can pass in a certain value and always get back
the same output from generate(). So we can easily create a unit test of generate(). If
we don't do this, the *global function* time() becomes a *dependency* of the generate()
function. And that sucks. ("*That sucks*" summarizes about 100 pages from *xUnit Test
Patterns* by Gerard Meszaros (Addison-Wesley); refer to that book if you want to understand this in more depth.)

Fine-Grained Timestamps

When you run *fx_server.seconds.php* from the command line, you will see something
like this:

```
data:{"timestamp":"2014-02-28 06:49:55","symbol":"AUD\/GBP","bid":"1.47219", ↵
    "ask":"1.47239"}

data:{"timestamp":"2014-02-28 06:49:56","symbol":"USD\/JPY","bid":"94.956", ↵
    "ask":"94.966"}

data:{"timestamp":"2014-02-28 06:49:56","symbol":"EUR\/USD","bid":"1.30931", ↵
    "ask":"1.30941"}

data:{"timestamp":"2014-02-28 06:49:57","symbol":"EUR\/USD","bid":"1.30983", ↵
    "ask":"1.30993"}

data:{"timestamp":"2014-02-28 06:49:57","symbol":"EUR\/USD","bid":"1.30975", ↵
    "ask":"1.30985"}

data:{"timestamp":"2014-02-28 06:49:57","symbol":"AUD\/GBP","bid":"1.47235", ↵
    "ask":"1.47255"}

data:{"timestamp":"2014-02-28 06:49:58","symbol":"AUD\/GBP","bid":"1.47129", ↵
    "ask":"1.47149"}
```

This data looks nice and random, doesn't it? But if you watch it for long enough you
will spot the long and short cycles we programmed in. Notice that EUR/USD has two
entries with the same timestamp. What we will do next is incorporate milliseconds into
our timestamps.

We only need to make these changes to our code:

1. In our main loop, use microtime(true) instead of time().
2. In generate(), include milliseconds in our formatted timestamp.

microtime(true) returns a float: the current timestamp in seconds since 1970 (just like
time() did) but to microsecond accuracy.

What about formatting our timestamp? What we currently have is:

```
'timestamp'=>gmdate("Y-m-d H:i:s",$t),
```

This still works. Even though $t is a floating point number, it is still seconds since 1970 and PHP will implicitly convert it to an int for the gmdate() function. So we just need to paste on the number of milliseconds.

We can get that number with ($t*1000)%1000 (multiply by 1,000 to turn $t into milliseconds since 1970, then just get the last three digits), and then use sprintf to format it so it is always three digits, and preceded by a decimal point:

```
'timestamp'=>gmdate("Y-m-d H:i:s",$t).
  sprintf(".%03d",($t*1000)%1000),
```

Here is the full version of the new FXPair class:

```php
<?php
class FXPair{
  /** The name of the FX pair */
  private $symbol;
  /** The mean bid price */
  private $bid;
  /** The spread. Add to $bid to get "ask" */
  private $spread;
  /** Accuracy to quote prices to */
  private $decimalPlaces;
  /** Number of seconds for one bigger cycle */
  private $longCycle;
  /** Number of seconds for the small cycle */
  private $shortCycle;

  /** Constructor */
  public function __construct($symbol,$b,$s,$d,$c1,$c2){
    $this->symbol = $symbol;
    $this->bid = $b;
    $this->spread = $s;
    $this->decimalPlaces = $d;
    $this->longCycle = $c1;
    $this->shortCycle = $c2;
  }

  /** @param float $t Seconds since 1970, to microsecond accuracy */
  public function generate($t){
$bid = $this->bid;
$bid += $this->spread * 100 *
  sin( (360 / $this->longCycle) * (deg2rad($t % $this->longCycle)) );
$bid += $this->spread * 30 *
  sin( (360 / $this->shortCycle) *(deg2rad($t % $this->shortCycle)) );
$bid += (mt_rand(-1000,1000)/1000.0) * 10 * $this->spread;
$ask = $bid + $this->spread;
```

```php
    return array(
      "timestamp" => gmdate("Y-m-d H:i:s",$t).
          sprintf(".%03d", ($t*1000)%1000),
      "symbol" => $this->symbol,
      "bid" => number_format($bid, $this->decimalPlaces),
      "ask" => number_format($ask, $this->decimalPlaces),
      );
    }

}
```

And here is the *fx_server.milliseconds.php* script that uses it:

```php
<?php
include_once("fxpair.milliseconds.php");

header("Content-Type: text/event-stream");

$symbols = array(
  new FXPair("EUR/USD", 1.3030, 0.0001, 5, 360, 47),
  new FXPair("EUR/USD", 1.3030, 0.0001, 5, 360, 47),
  new FXPair("USD/JPY", 95.10, 0.01, 3, 341, 55),
  new FXPair("AUD/GBP", 1.455, 0.0002, 5, 319, 39),
  );

while(true){
  $sleepSecs = mt_rand(250,500)/1000.0;
  usleep( $sleepSecs * 1000000 );

  $t = microtime(true);
  $ix = mt_rand(0,count($symbols)-1);
  $d = $symbols[$ix]->generate($t);
  echo "data:".json_encode($d)."\n\n";
  @ob_flush();@flush();
  }
```

When we run *fx_server.milliseconds.php*, we now see something like this:

```
data:{"timestamp":"2014-02-28 06:49:55.081","symbol":"AUD\/GBP", ↵
    "bid":"1.47219","ask":"1.47239"}

data:{"timestamp":"2014-02-28 06:49:56.222","symbol":"USD\/JPY", ↵
    "bid":"94.956","ask":"94.966"}

data:{"timestamp":"2014-02-28 06:49:56.790","symbol":"EUR\/USD", ↵
    "bid":"1.30931","ask":"1.30941"}

data:{"timestamp":"2014-02-28 06:49:57.002","symbol":"EUR\/USD", ↵
    "bid":"1.30983","ask":"1.30993"}

data:{"timestamp":"2014-02-28 06:49:57.450","symbol":"EUR\/USD", ↵
    "bid":"1.30972","ask":"1.30982"}
```

```
data:{"timestamp":"2014-02-28 06:49:57.987","symbol":"AUD\/GBP", ↵
    "bid":"1.47235","ask":"1.47255"}

data:{"timestamp":"2014-02-28 06:49:58.345","symbol":"AUD\/GBP", ↵
    "bid":"1.47129","ask":"1.47149"}
```

In the book's source code, there is a file called *fx_client.basic.milliseconds.html* that allows you to view this in the browser (Figure 3-2). Each time you run the script you will see the three currencies going up and down, and if watching paint dry is one of your hobbies you will probably quite enjoy this. And as long as you don't mind watching it for at least six minutes (the length of the long cycle), this is also good enough for manual testing. But each time you run the script, the exact prices, the order in which the symbols appear, and of course the timestamps, are different. Refer back to "Design for Testability" on page 31 for why we want to do something about this.

USD/JPY	EUR/USD	AUD/GBP
94.628	1.30016	

Figure 3-2. fx_client with milliseconds, after running for a few seconds

Taking Control of the Randomness

 The rest of this chapter is only backend enhancements; if you are more interested in the frontend, you could skip ahead to Chapter 4 now.

As an experiment, take your *fx_server.milliseconds.php* script and at the top add this one line: `mt_srand(123);`. This sets the *random seed* to a value of your choosing.

Stop it. Run it again. What do you notice? If you thought setting the seed would give you repeatable results, that must have come as a nasty shock. Everything is different. But look closely, and you'll see the order of the ticking symbols is consistent: EUR/USD three times, then USD/JPY, then AUD/GBP, then USD/JPY three times.[3] That makes

---

3. The exact random sequence, for a given seed, might change between PHP versions, and possibly between OSes. I used PHP 5.3 on 64-bit Linux when writing this.

sense because the code to control the next symbol is simple randomness: `$ix = mt_rand(0,count($symbols)-1);`.

If you look *really* closely, you'll also see that the difference between timestamps is *almost* the same. For example, I see a gap of 431ms on one run, 430ms on another run, and 431ms on a third try. This also makes sense because the time between ticks is also simple randomness: `$sleepSecs=mt_rand(250,500)*1000;`. The difference in timing is due to CPU speed, how busy the machine is at the time, and the flapping of the wings of a butterfly on the other side of Earth.

But why are the prices different? Because they are based on `$t` (the current time on the server), with just a little random noise added in. So we need to take control of `$t`. Now, was your first thought, "Let's change the system clock, just before running each unit test"? I like your style. You are a useful person to have around when we have a wall to get through and the only tool we have is a sledgehammer. To be honest, I thought of it too.

But in this case there is an easier way to get through this wall—there is a door. And it was us who put it there earlier. I am talking about the way we pass `$t` to `generate()`, rather than having `generate()` call `microtime(true)` itself.

Just to get a feel for this, replace the `$t = microtime(true);` line with `$t=1234567890.0;`. Now it outputs:

```
data:{"timestamp":"2009-02-13 23:31:30.000","symbol":"EUR\/USD",↵
    "bid":"1.31103","ask":"1.31113"}
```

And it is that exact same line every time you run the script, regardless of the CPU, load, or insect behavior.

Obviously we do not want it to be February 13, 2009 forever. Here is the next version of our code, which gives us the option to take control of `$t`:

```php
<?php
include_once("fxpair.milliseconds.php");

header("Content-Type: text/event-stream");

$symbols = array(
  new FXPair("EUR/USD", 1.3030, 0.0001, 5, 360, 47),
  new FXPair("EUR/USD", 1.3030, 0.0001, 5, 360, 47),
  new FXPair("USD/JPY", 95.10, 0.01, 3, 341, 55),
  new FXPair("AUD/GBP", 1.455, 0.0002, 5, 319, 39),
  );

if(isset($argc) && $argc>=2)
    $t = $argv[1];
elseif(array_key_exists("seed",$_REQUEST))
    $t = $_REQUEST["seed"];
else{
```

```
    $t = microtime(true);
    echo "data:{\"seed\":$t}\n\n";
    }
  mt_srand($t*1000);

  while(true){
    $sleepSecs = mt_rand(250,500)/1000.0;
    usleep( $sleepSecs * 1000000 );
    $t += $sleepSecs;

    $ix = mt_rand(0,count($symbols)-1);
    $d = $symbols[$ix]->generate($t);
    echo "data:".json_encode($d)."\n\n";
    @ob_flush();@flush();
    }
```

Compared to *fx_server.milliseconds.php*, the main change is the block of code just before the main loop. But, in fact, the code is quite mundane. If run from the command line (if(isset($argc)...), it gets the seed from the first command-line parameter; if run from a web server, it looks for input[4] called seed and uses that ($_REQUEST['seed'];). And when neither are set, it initializes from the current time, and then it outputs a line to say what seed it is using. This last point is so that if something goes wrong you have the seed to reproduce the stream of data. Once we've got our random seed, we call mt_srand from one of those three places. We multiply $t by 1,000; mt_srand will truncate it to an int, so this is our way of saying we care about millisecond accuracy, but not microsecond accuracy.

In our main loop, the changes are simple. $t=microtime(true); has been removed from the start of the loop, and at the end of the loop, $t is incremented by the number of seconds we slept. In other words, if $t is 1234567890.0, meaning we are pretending it is 2009-02-13 23:31:30.000, and then we sleep for 0.325 seconds, we update $t such that we now pretend the current time is 2009-02-13 23:31:30.325.

Making Allowance for the Real Passage of Time

What a fun section title! As far as unit testing goes, the code at the end of the previous section is good enough. But did you try using it without a random seed? To make what is happening clear, I added this[5] just above the line that starts echo "data:"...:

---

4. Yes, I'm using $_REQUEST deliberately, so it can come from GET, POST, or even cookie data. In this particular case, being able to set the random seed from a cookie is a feature, not a bug! See "Superglobals" on page 198 in Appendix C for more on PHP superglobals.

5. You'll find this in the book's source code as *fx_server.repeatable_with_datestamp.php*.

```php
$now=microtime(true);
echo ":".
  gmdate("Y-m-d H:i:s",$now).
  sprintf(".%03d",($now*1000)%1000).
  "\n";
```

Starting a line with a colon is a way to enter a comment in SSE. You cannot access comments from a browser, so run this from the command line. At the start, you will see $now and $t are in sync. But after a few ticks, $now might be a few milliseconds slower. Go put the kettle on, and when you come back the gap will be in the hundreds of milliseconds. Run it for 24 hours and it will be minutes wrong. (By the way, the problem exists when you give a seed too; it is just harder to spot.)

Well, it is just test data, it doesn't really matter. But adjusting sleep to match the passage of time is a tool you might need in your toolbox, so let's quickly do it.

We will use a variable, $clock, to store the server clock time. That is initialized to the current time at the start of our script. But the real action is at the end of the main loop. $now=microtime(true); is back! Then we calculate the time slip with $adjustment = $now - $clock;. The key concept is when we go to sleep, we sleep for a bit less than we thought we wanted to:

```php
usleep( ($sleepSecs - $adjustment) * 1000000);
```

$t is updated as before, i.e., $sleepSecs without using $adjustment. But then we also update $clock in exactly the same way. $clock represents the time we expect the server clock to have if we are running on an infinitely fast processor.

The full code for *fx_server.adjusting.php* is shown in the following code block, and you can find *fx_server.adjusting_with_datestamp.php* in the book's source code, which uses SSE comments again to show that the artificial data is spit out at exactly the same pace as the real passage of time. You will also find *fx_client.basic.adjusting.html*, which connects to it (this version displays the seed that was chosen), and *fx_client.basic.adjusting123.html*, which sets an explicit seed, and thus shows repeatable data each time you reload.

```php
<?php
include_once("fxpair.milliseconds.php");

header("Content-Type: text/event-stream");

$symbols = array(
  new FXPair('EUR/USD', 1.3030, 0.0001, 5, 360, 47),
  new FXPair('EUR/USD', 1.3030, 0.0001, 5, 360, 47),
  new FXPair('USD/JPY', 95.10, 0.01, 3, 341, 55),
  new FXPair('AUD/GBP', 1.455, 0.0002, 5, 319, 39),
  );

$clock = microtime(true);
```

```
if(isset($argc) && $argc>=2)
    $t = $argv[1];
elseif(array_key_exists('seed',$_REQUEST))
    $t = $_REQUEST['seed'];
else{
    $t = $clock;
    echo "data:{\"seed\":$t}\n\n";
    }
mt_srand($t*1000);

while(true){
  $sleepSecs = mt_rand(250,500)/1000.0;
  $now = microtime(true);
  $adjustment = $now - $clock;

  usleep( ($sleepSecs - $adjustment) * 1000000 );
  $t += $sleepSecs;
  $clock += $sleepSecs;

  $ix = mt_rand(0,count($symbols)-1);
  $d = $symbols[$ix]->generate($t);
  echo "data:".json_encode($d)."\n\n";
  @ob_flush();@flush();
  }
```

Taking Stock

We covered a lot of ground in this chapter. Step by step, we designed a random data backend that incorporates Design for Testability principles (while learning a little about how FX markets work), then pushed that data to clients using SSE. But our development was quite rapid, so the next chapter will start with some refactoring, and then it will add some data storage features.

CHAPTER 4

Living in More Than the Present Moment

We are doing well. We now have a fairly sophisticated server, which is relatively easy to test, and a basic frontend so at least we can see it is working. It is almost time to restore the balance and improve that frontend, too. But before we return our attention back to the frontend, there is one more change I want to make on the backend. It is a change to the structure of our data, and therefore will break compatibility with the *fx_client.ba sic.*.html* files we've seen previously.

More Structure in Our Data

Currently each JSON record is one tick, one item of data. The main change we will make is in allowing multiple rows of data to be passed. We also had a couple of "header" fields: one the name of the symbol, the other a server timestamp. So our data structure will become like this:

symbol:string

timestamp:string ("YYYY-MM-DD HH:MM:SS.sss")

rows:array

And each row in the `rows` container has this structure:

timestamp:string ("YYYY-MM-DD HH:MM:SS.sss")

bid:double

ask:double

Why are we doing this? One reason is to be ready for if/when we have arrays of data to send (for instance, supporting historical data requests). Of course, we could just send each row as its own row of JSON; doing it that way adds a few bytes, perhaps a dozen bytes per row. A better reason is we are telling the client this is a logical block of data. Our message callback is called for each SSE message we send; chances are your application will update the display after each. If we send a few hundred rows as a block, the client can process them as a block, and then just update the display once at the end.

Another reason for doing this is that it gives us a bit more flexibility. We could add a type field to change the meaning of rows, perhaps to say it is gzipped CSV, not a JSON array. It allows us to add a version number. Who knows what we will want to do in the future?[1]

After all that chat, the code for the change is quite small; it only affects the `gener ate()` function in our `FXPair` class. Relative to *fxpair.milliseconds.php*, the second half of the `generate()` function in *fxpair.structured.php* looks like this:

```
$ts = gmdate("Y-m-d H:i:s",$t).sprintf(".%03d", ($t*1000)%1000);
return array(
  "symbol" => $this->symbol,
  "timestamp" => $ts,
  "rows" => array(
    array(
      "timestamp" => $ts,
      "bid" => number_format($bid, $this->decimal_places),
      "ask" => number_format($ask, $this->decimal_places),
    )
  )
);
```

 In PHP, an array with named keys is called an associative array; it will become an object in the JSON. An array with no keys (as here), or numeric keys, will become an array in the JSON.

Notice that I set the timestamp of the message, and the timestamp of the data, to be the same. They need not be the same, though: the timestamp in the rows might have come from a stock exchange and have the official exchange timestamp on it, so it might be a few milliseconds earlier than the message timestamp. Or if it is historical data, it might be months or years earlier.

Refactoring the PHP

The PHP script is under 40 lines, so there is not really that much to refactor. But I'm betting that seeing this block of code over and over is starting to set your teeth on edge:

---

1. We already did this earlier, in an ad hoc way, when we sent an SSE message that specifies the chosen seed and nothing else.

```
$d = $symbols[$ix]->generate($t);
echo "data:".json_encode($d)."\n\n";
@ob_flush();@flush();
```

So I will replace it with this:

```
sendData($symbols[$ix]->generate($t));
```

And the implementation of sendData() is simple:

```
function sendData($data){
echo "data:";
echo json_encode($data)."\n";
echo "\n";
@flush();@ob_flush();
}
```

(Splitting it into three echo commands is not actually to make it fit this book's formatting; it is ready for the change we will make in Chapter 6. Here is a hint: the middle line is the actual data, whereas the "data:" prefix and the extra LF are the SSE protocol.)

You can see this change in the book's source code: *fx_server.structured.php*; the only other change is to include *fxpair.structured.php* instead of *fxpair.milliseconds.php*.

Refactoring the JavaScript

Our current JavaScript is all of six lines. But to take this further, it will help to have some structure; some of the design decisions we make here are also preparing the way for the fallbacks for older browsers.

First up, we need a couple of globals:

```
var url = "fx_server.structured.php?";
var es = null;
```

 Why do we put the question mark at the end of the URL? Later we will want to append values to the URL, and doing it this way allows us to append without having to know if we are the first parameter (which has to be prefixed with ?) or one of the later ones (which need to be prefixed with &).

We would like to move the call to create the EventSource object into a function called startEventSource(), which looks like this:

```
function startEventSource(){
if(es)es.close();
es = new EventSource(url);
es.addEventListener("message", function(e){processOneLine(e.data);}, false);
es.addEventListener("error", handleError, false);
}
```

We will write that handleError function in the next chapter; for the moment, just write:

```
function handleError(e){}
```

Next we are going to wrap the call to startEventSource() in a function called con
nect, so it looks like this:

```
function connect(){
if(window.EventSource)startEventSource();
//else handle fallbacks here
}
```

You may have heard that all problems in programming can be solved by adding another layer of indirection. Well, obviously we are adding a layer of abstraction here…so what is the problem we are solving? Again it is for the fallback support: code that will be used by all techniques (e.g., keep-alive) goes in connect(), as well as the detection of which technique to use. Code specific to using SSE goes in startEventSource().

Then, to get everything rolling, we will call connect() once the page has loaded. The simplest way is to put this code in a <script> block at the very bottom of the page:

```
setTimeout(connect, 100);
```

If you are using JQuery, the following way may be more familiar (and you can put this code anywhere if done this way; it does not need to go at the bottom):

```
$(function(){ setTimeout(connect, 100); });
```

 We use a 0.1s timeout because some versions of some browsers need it. For instance, on some versions of Safari, without using a timeout you might see a permanent "loading" animation. I hate the "magic number" of 100ms, but it appears to be sufficient.

The other refactor we did was to move our processing to its own function, process
OneLine(s), which takes a single line of JSON as the parameter:

```
function processOneLine(s){
var d = JSON.parse(s);
if(d.seed){
  var x = document.getElementById("seed");
  x.innerHTML += "seed=" + d.seed;
  }
else if(d.symbol){
  var x = document.getElementById(d.symbol);
  for(var ix in d.rows){
    var r = d.rows[ix];
    x.innerHTML = r.bid;
    }
  }
}
```

This function also shows how we handle the change in the JSON format, described in the previous section. I am using a loop here to show how to process each row in the received data. In this case, each row updates the same div so, effectively, only the last row of data is being used. But most of the time you will care about all the data, and want to use a loop.

See *fx_client.basic.structured.html* for the file after all this refactoring. It behaves exactly like the previous version (*fx_client.basic.adjusting.html*), the goal of any good refactoring session. Never mix adding features with refactoring.

By the way, when you are actually only interested in the final row of data, that whole block can be written as:

```
var x = document.getElementById(d.symbol);
x.innerHTML = d.rows[ d.rows.length - 1 ].bid;
```

You can do this because d.rows is an array, not an object. If d.rows was an object (e.g., with timestamps as the keys) you would always have to use the loop. Speaking of which, because d.rows is an array, you could also write the main loop this way:

```
for(var ix = 0;ix < d.rows.length;++ix){
  var r = d.rows[ix];
  x.innerHTML = r.bid;
  }
```

Adding a History Store

In our application, we currently use each value as we get it, but then we forget about it. If we instead keep a record of everything we receive, it creates new possibilities. For instance, we could make a tabular view of all data received in the last 5 minutes or 24 hours. Or we could make a chart.

Let's start by adding this global variable to store the history for all our symbols:

```
var fullHistory = {};
```

It is an object in JavaScript, but we will use it as an associative array (aka map, dictionary, hash, key-value pair store); the *key* will be the symbol name, and the *value* will be another associative array. Then when we get a line of data (one JSON record, which contains one or more rows of data), we do:

```
if(!fullHistory.hasOwnProperty(d.symbol))
  fullHistory[d.symbol] = {};
```

That just creates an entry (an empty JavaScript object) for a particular feed, the first time we see it. Then, to fill it, we use something like:

```
for(var ix in d.rows){
    var r = d.rows[ix];
    fullHistory[d.symbol][r.key] = r.value;
    }
```

That code snippet assumes a key field and a value field in each row. In our code r.timestamp will be the key, and the value will be set to an array of two values: [r.bid,r.ask]. So, in full, our new processOneLine(s) function becomes:

```
function processOneLine(s){
var d = JSON.parse(s);
if(d.seed){
  var x = document.getElementById("seed");
  x.innerHTML += "seed=" + d.seed;
  }
else if(d.symbol){
  if(!fullHistory.hasOwnProperty(d.symbol))fullHistory[d.symbol] = {};
  var x = document.getElementById(d.symbol);
  for(var ix in d.rows){
    var r = d.rows[ix];
    x.innerHTML = d.rows[ix].bid;
    fullHistory[d.symbol][r.timestamp] = [r.bid,r.ask];
    }
  update_history_table(d.symbol);
  }
}
```

If we want to take that history store, and show the most recent 10 items as an HTML table for one of the symbols, how do we do it? The following function makes a table for one symbol:

```
function makeHistoryTbody(history){
var tbody = document.createElement("tbody");
var keys = Object.keys(history).sort().slice(-10).reverse();

var timestamp, v, row, cell;
for(var n = 0;n < keys.length;n++){
    timestamp = keys[n];
    v = history[timestamp];
    row = document.createElement("tr");

    cell = document.createElement("th");
    cell.appendChild(document.createTextNode(timestamp));
    row.appendChild(cell);

    cell = document.createElement("td");
    cell.appendChild(document.createTextNode(v[0]));
    row.appendChild(cell);

    cell = document.createElement("td");
    cell.appendChild(document.createTextNode(v[1]));
    row.appendChild(cell);
```

```
        tbody.appendChild(row);
    }
    return tbody;
}
```

So we create an HTML DOM `tbody` object, then grab the keys of the most recent 10 entries in our data history. (The `reverse()` at the end puts the most recent quote at the top of our table.) Then we loop through them, create a table row for them, append three table cells to the row, and then append the row to the `tbody`, which we return.

The final link is to replace the currently displayed `tbody` with our new one. This function does that:

```
function updateHistoryTable(symbol){
var tbody = makeHistoryTbody(fullHistory[symbol]);
var x = document.getElementById("history_" + symbol);
x.parentNode.replaceChild(tbody, x);
tbody.id = x.id;
}
```

The final file, *fx_client.history.html*, uses some CSS and some responsive web design principles so it will look good and use the space effectively on both mobile and desktop. Figures 4-1, 4-2, and 4-3 show how it looks just after being loaded, after a few seconds, and after running for a while, respectively.

Figure 4-1. fx_client.history.html, just after starting

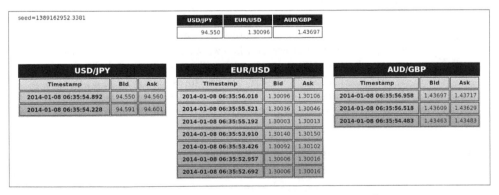

Figure 4-2. fx_client.history.html, after running for about 5 seconds

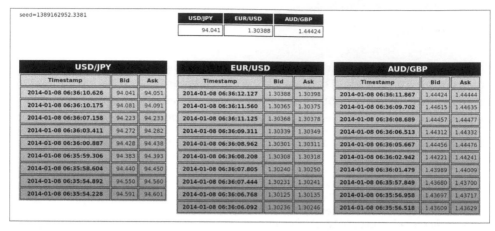

Figure 4-3. fx_client.history.html, after running for some time

I'm not going to go into the CSV and web design, because it is off-topic for this book, but let's just look at one of the three tables:

```
<table class="price-table">
  <caption>USD/JPY</caption>
  <thead>
    <tr>
      <th>Timestamp</th>
      <th>Bid</th>
      <th>Ask</th>
    </tr>
  </thead>
  <tbody id="history_USD/JPY"></tbody>
</table>
```

Each table has a static caption and header, and then we give the tbody an id so that we can find it and replace just that part of the table.

 Object.keys is available in all browsers where SSE is also available, so no problem there. However, when we start adding fallbacks we will need a polyfill for IE8 and earlier. We will introduce the polyfill when we first need it. Be aware that the polyfill is slower: it is an O(n) algorithm (where n is the number of keys), whereas a native Object.keys should be O(1).

One final word of caution: as you watch this page chug away, busily updating itself, remember we are deliberately only showing the last 10 quotes for each symbol. But we are storing *all* the quotes ever received in memory. You need to balance functionality against the client's resources (available memory in this case). If you know you'll never need them all, consider truncating the `fullHistory` object at regular intervals.

Persistent Storage

The previous section showed how we can store all the data that is streamed to us, opening up a world of possibilities: tables, real-time charts, client-side analysis using the latest machine learning technologies, and so on. You could be beating the markets without ever having to leave the browser...until you close the browser, that is. Then all that downloaded data, and all your calculations, disappear down the drain.

HTML5 technologies to the rescue! In fact, we have a choice. However, FileSystem is not widely implemented yet, and neither is IndexedDB (though a polyfill is available that extends its reach a bit). So we will go with Web Storage. Some common restrictions for all of these new HTML5 storage APIs is that the user's permission is needed to approve the storage, and that the storage is by *origin*. We will look at the exact definition of an origin in Chapter 9, but the idea is that an application running at *http://example.com/* cannot see data created by an application running at *http://other.site/*.

Web Storage is more commonly known as `localStorage`. This allows us to store name/value pairs, and typically browsers will give an application 5MB of storage. The best thing about Web Storage is it is available just about everywhere—IE8 onward (polyfill available for IE6 and IE7), Firefox since 3.5, Chrome since forever, Safari4 onward, Android 2.1 onward, and Opera 10.5 onward (see the *Can I Use Web Storage?* page (*http://caniuse.com/namevalue-storage*)).

The downside is that it doesn't take structured data, only strings. This means our history object has to be converted to a string using `JSON.stringify()`. That is a bit inefficient, and if we start to deal with lots of data, there is also the memory and CPU time required to convert between them.

The code to use Web Storage is quite straightforward, requiring just two changes to our existing code. First, to save the data, insert this line in `processOneLine(s)`:

```
function processOneLine(s){
var d = JSON.parse(s);
...
else if(d.symbol){
  if(!fullHistory.hasOwnProperty(d.symbol))fullHistory[d.symbol] = {};
  ...
  updateHistoryTable(d.symbol);
  localStorage.fullHistory = JSON.stringify(fullHistory);
  }
}
```

Yes, it is that simple. `JSON.stringify()` turns our `fullHistory` object into a string. The assignment to `localStorage.XXX` either creates the XXX key or replaces it. You could also write this as `localStorage.setItem("fullHistory", JSON.stringify(fullHistory));`.

Be aware of what is happening here: every time a single piece of data comes through, our entire history is being turned into a string, replacing what is already there. In one of my tests, after an hour or so Firefox was using 25% of one CPU (compared to 4% at the start), and the string being made was 500KB in length. Those aren't fatal numbers, but after a few more hours they would be.

Optimizations

There are two independent optimizations possible. You could split the data by symbol. So the line would change to:

```
localStorage.setItem("fullHistory." + d.symbol,
    JSON.stringify( fullHistory[d.symbol]) );
```

We have three symbols, so this means each string is 1/3 of the original size, which effectively means if the failure point was previously 4 hours, it is now 12 hours. You could take this idea further by putting part of the datestamp in the key name. For example, each hour's data could end up in its own bucket. This adds quite a bit of complexity though, because you now will need another `localStorage` entry to keep track of which time periods you have data stored for. (Alternatively, the `localStorage` API provides a way to iterate through *all* stored data: `for(var ix = 0; ix < localStorage.length; ix++){var key = localStorage.key(i); ... }`.)

The other optimization is to save the data on a 30-second timer using `setInterval`, instead of each time we get data. This definitely reduces overall CPU usage, but remember that instead of, say, a constant 100% CPU usage, after a certain amount of time, you will get a 100% CPU burst every 30 seconds. The other thing to remember is that when the browser closes, then up to 30 seconds worth of data gets lost.

The other change needed in our code is to use the persistent storage. At the top of `connect()` these lines are added:

```
function connect(){
if(localStorage.fullHistory){
    fullHistory = JSON.parse(localStorage.fullHistory);
    updateHistoryTable("USD/JPY");
    updateHistoryTable("EUR/USD");
    updateHistoryTable("AUD/GBP");
    }
if(window.EventSource)startEventSource();
//else handle fallbacks here
}
```

This is simply the reverse of how the data was saved, using JSON.parse instead of JSON.stringify. It could also have been written fullHistory = JSON.parse(local Storage.getItem("fullHistory"));.

The other three lines update the display with the previously stored data.

If it does not work, check your browser settings. In some browsers the policy of what is allowed is shared with cookies, so you may need to allow cookies to be stored too. If it is working when you click the browser's reload button, but not working after closing all browser windows, check for privacy settings that say all cookies should be deleted at the end of a browser session.

 To delete the data, it is as simple as localStorage.removeItem('full History');. If you implemented the idea of splitting the data into hourly buckets, mentioned in the sidebar "Optimizations" on page 56, then you could use this to just delete the oldest data.

How much data can you store? It is browser-specific, but generally you can expect at least 5MB (about 11 to 12 hours for our FX demo application). What happens when you reach the limit? Typically the setItem() call will fail, throwing a QUOTA_EXCEE DED_ERR exception that you could catch and deal with. The previously stored data for that key is kept. The Opera browser will first pop up a dialog giving the user the chance to allow more storage. Firefox has the dom.storage.default_quota key (found in about:config), which a user could first edit.

How to Reduce the Size of the Data?

One idea is to compress the JSON string before storing it. A web search will find zip, gzip, and LZW implementations in JavaScript. JSON compresses well.

You could also try summarizing the data instead of storing the raw data. This is lossy compression, rather than the lossless compression suggestions of the previous paragraph. For instance, in a finance application, it is very common to turn raw ticks into bars. So a one-minute bar will just store the opening price, closing price, high and low price, and the volume or number of ticks for each 60-second period. With some careful planning you can have almost constant space usage. For instance, you could store 10 minutes of raw data, two hours' worth of one-minute bars, one week's worth of hourly bars, and years worth of daily bars.

The downside to both ideas is the extra CPU load and the extra complexity.

Now We Are Historians...

This chapter started by improving the structure of the code that Chapter 3 left us with. Then we built on our new base to learn how to store a history, and display both the latest prices and a subset of that history. Then we looked at how to integrate this with another HTML5 technology, Web Storage, so clients can have a persistent data cache. We are now done with features, and the next chapter is all about making our application *production-quality*.

CHAPTER 5

No More Ivory Tower: Making Our Application Production-Quality

In the previous couple of chapters we created a backend that pushes out FX prices for multiple symbols, and a frontend that displays them in any browser that supports SSE. One way we need to improve this application is by getting it to work in older desktop and mobile browsers that do not have SSE support. But there is another axis we need to improve in, because at the moment I still regard this as a *toy example*. It is not production-quality yet.

What do I mean by production-quality? Quite a few things. I mean that when things go wrong the system will recover automatically. I mean it works with real-world constraints (the one we will show in this chapter is dealing with the FX market shutting down on weekends). And I mean dealing with the case where we sent out bad data by mistake and now need to fix it.

Error Handling

In Chapter 4, we attached an event handler for the `error` message. We named that function `handleError`, and now we have to decide what is going to go into it. By the end of this chapter we will be auto-reconnecting whenever the backend server goes down. We will also keep trying to connect if it is not available. But we will be doing these things with or without an `error` callback. The `error` callback is just informative—only of interest to programmers, not to end users. So we might as well make it as simple as:

```
function handleError(e){
console.log(e);
}
```

I said "informative." I was exaggerating. The object has no message, no error code. The only slightly useful thing is the `target` element. This is your `EventSource` object. Inside it you will find the URL you connected to, and an element called `readyState` (or, in full, `e.target.readyState`). If `readyState` is 2, it means "CLOSED." This means your URL is bad— a connection could not be made. If `readyState` is 0, it means "CONNECTING," and that means you had a connection, but it got closed and the browser is trying to auto-reconnect. And if `readyState` is 1, or "OPEN," by the time you look at it, it means the reconnect already happened.

Bad JSON

If the server sends a JSON string that isn't a JSON string, or is badly formatted (sometimes even as much as a stray comma or line feed), the browser might throw an exception. This will stop everything from working. And that is bad. So, instead of just writing `var d = JSON.parse(s);`, this is the production-quality approach:

```
try{
  var d = JSON.parse(s);
}catch(e){
  console.log("BAD JSON:" + s + "\n" + e);
  return;
}
```

Adding Keep-Alive

I can sometimes go weeks, even months, without any really important news I need to tell Mum. But how can she tell the difference between me having no news, me forgetting to pay my ISP and phone company, and me having been hit by a fiery comet and lying in a hospital? So, every now and again I email Mum to tell her: "Bills paid, no fiery comets." Or more simply: "I'm alive."

In network terms, keep-alive is a packet of data that is sent every N seconds, or after N seconds of inactivity on a socket, just to let the other end of the socket know that everything is OK and that there simply hasn't been anything to communicate. (You will also see this concept referred to as a heartbeat.) Some browsers might kill a connection and auto-reconnect after so many seconds of socket inactivity. In addition, proxy servers might kill a connection if it goes quiet. So we're going to send keep-alive messages every 15 seconds to prevent this from happening. Why 15? The SSE draft proposal mentions that number. It is probably more frequent than is really needed, but on the other hand, it is not frequent enough to ever likely be the bottleneck of your system.

So, that decides N. The other design decision we have is whether we send the keep-alive *every* 15 seconds, or only after 15 seconds of quiet. It is not a very important decision, so I suggest you do whichever is easiest to code on the server side for you.

Be aware that keep-alives could affect TCP/IP bandwidth shaping, and in particular its Slow-Start Restart mechanism. My advice: don't worry about it. If the difference between a 15-second, 30-second, or 90-second SSE keep-alive is having a significant effect on your network load, there could be bigger problems elsewhere. (For starters, why do you have so many SSE connections that are not sending any real data?) Alternatively, you could configure your server to not use slow-start (it is an OS-level setting).

With mobile, keep-alive brings other considerations. For instance, the keep-alive might be stopping the application from going to sleep, thus draining the battery rapidly. If your data is naturally infrequent, but is also predictable, consider using setTimeout to fetch data, instead of streaming it.

Server Side

The keep-alive can be as simple as sending a blank SSE comment line. How do we do that? It is just a line that starts with a colon. You may remember we used SSE comments to add some troubleshooting output in the section "Making Allowance for the Real Passage of Time" on page 44. Here's an example:

```
echo ":\n\n";@flush();@ob_flush();
```

Alternatively, we could send a blank data message:

```
echo "data:\n\n";@flush();@ob_flush();
```

What is the difference between sending an SSE comment line and sending an SSE data line? On the server side it is four bytes, but on the client side there is all the difference in the world. The latter triggers the EventSource message handler, and the former does not.[1] We want the latter, for reasons we will cover later when talking about client-side handling.

So, if we are going to send a real data packet, let's also include a timestamp (this can then be used to identify clocks that are out of sync or suspiciously large latency between server and client). Because we are using JSON for our messages, it is no trouble to also identify the message as a keep-alive, as follows:

```
sendData( array(
  "action" => "keep-alive",
  "timestamp" => gmdate("Y-m-d H:i:s")
) );
```

You can find an example using this in the sample code for the book: *fx_server.keepa live.php*. Because our application is constantly sending data, there would never be 15 seconds of quiet, and so we would never get chance to send a keep-alive. (Basically, the

---

1. At the time of writing, all browsers quietly swallow SSE comments, so you cannot even see them in the developer tools.

keep-alive concept is pointless for our particular application.) But to allow us to test it on the frontend, we use the *regular send* pattern. We do this by initializing `$nextKeepalive = time() + 15;` just before entering the main infinite loop. Simply put, that line says send the next keep-alive message 15 seconds from now. Then the start of the main loop, just after the sleep, now looks like:

```
while(true){
  ...
  if(time() > $nextKeepalive){
    sendData( array(
      "action" => "keep-alive",
      "timestamp" => gmdate("Y-m-d H:i:s")
      ) );
    $nextKeepalive = time() + 15;
    }
  $ix = mt_rand(0, count($symbols)-1 );
  ...
```

To change it to only send after quiet periods, simply run `$nextKeepalive = time() + 15;` after sending real data too.

Client Side

SSE already has a reconnect function built into the protocol. So, in that sense, we don't strictly need keep-alive handling. Just sending an SSE comment (see the previous section) will be enough to keep the TCP/IP socket alive. And if that socket dies, the browser should automatically reconnect. There are two reasons we choose not to rely on that functionality. The first is that the browser will only reconnect if the socket dies nice and cleanly and immediately, like an extra in an action movie. However, sometimes sockets can die like the hero in an action movie. And just like in the movie, it might be 30, 60, or even 120 seconds from when the socket stops working to the browser being sure it is dead. Bugs in your backend code can cause a similar problem. The second reason is nice and simple: we want our code to work with the fallbacks, too. That is why we send a keep-alive as a proper message that can be processed in our JavaScript.

First we need to define a couple of global variables in our JavaScript:

```
var keepaliveSecs = 20;
var keepaliveTimer = null;
```

The first decides how sensitive we want to be. The correct value is to match the pace of the keep-alive messages that the backend sends. We chose 15 seconds for our backend; I like to add a bit of buffer, to allow for network latency and other delays on both the front and backends, which is why I have chosen 20 seconds.

`keepaliveTimer` is the handle of a `setTimer()` call. We create this timer when we do the initial connect. Then, whenever data comes through from the server we kill the old timer and create a new one. So, as long as data (whether real data or a keep-alive message) keeps coming through regularly, the timer will always be killed before it gets a chance to trigger. Only when no data comes through for a period of 20 seconds will the timer finally get a chance to trigger. And that can only mean there is a problem somewhere, because keep-alive messages are supposed to be received every 15 seconds.

In code that looks like this:

```
function gotActivity(){
if(keepaliveTimer != null)clearTimeout(keepaliveTimer);
keepaliveTimer = setTimeout(connect, keepaliveSecs * 1000);
}
```

The second parameter to setTimeout is given in milliseconds, hence the multiply by 1,000. The first parameter is the function to call after the timeout, so it will call connect() if no keep-alive is received. You remember that we have a function called connect that previously looked like this:

```
function connect(){
if(window.EventSource)startEventSource();
//else handle fallbacks here
}
```

To start things going we just add one line at the top, so it looks like:

```
function connect(){
gotActivity();
if(window.EventSource)startEventSource();
//else handle fallbacks here
}
```

This is very important: without it, a connection that went wrong (that never sent any data) would go unnoticed. It goes at the start just in case startEventSource() throws an exception, and the end of the function is not reached.

Are you concerned we don't kill the old connection in connect()? We leave that job to startEventSource() (and we already handle it: see "Refactoring the JavaScript" on page 49). The way to kill the connection varies depending on the fallback we are using.

There is one final piece to add. At the very top of processOneLine(s) we add a call to gotActivity():

```
function processOneLine(s){
gotActivity();
var d = JSON.parse(s);
...
```

It does not matter if it is a keep-alive, regular data, or anything else. Ending up in processOneLine(s) is a sign of getting a message. The fallbacks we look at in the next two chapters will also use connect() and processOneLine(s), so there will be no changes to this code for them to support keep-alives. Try out *fx_client.keepalive.html*

to see it in action; Figure 5-1 shows how it will look after a couple of keep-alives have
come through.

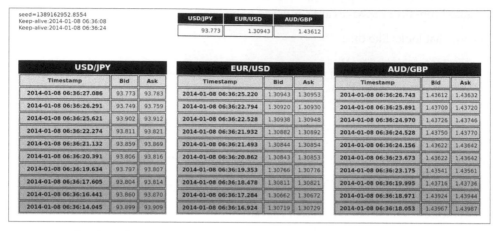

Figure 5-1. fx_client.keepalive.html after running for about 35 seconds; two keep-alives have come through

Another Way to Do Keep-Alives

Our current keep-alive solution kills and re-creates a timer every single time we get new data. An alternative approach is to just record the timestamp of the latest data. This then (for instance) could require a once-every-four-second timer. Each time that timer triggers, it checks to see how long it has been since we got real data; when that is over 20 seconds, it assumes that the server has died, at which point it can try to reconnect.

This approach has some downsides. It needs a couple more globals (`var keepaliveTi merSecs=4;`, `var lastTimestamp=null;`). It needs about double the number of lines of code. And it becomes less precise: when the server goes down it will be between 20 and 24 seconds before we notice. The way it was shown previously, we will notice exactly 20 seconds after the last received message.

There must be some advantage to doing it this way, right? Yes, updating a timestamp each time we get data is quicker than killing and starting a timer. This extra CPU load comes just when we want it least: when we are getting a burst of very rapid data, and already had more than enough to do, thank you very much for asking.

The first draft of this chapter did it this way in the main text, and the simpler version was in this sidebar. However, I got suspicious and went away to benchmark the difference. In Chrome (well, actually WebKit/PhantomJS), the stop-start of the timers took 14 to 17 times longer than just assigning the current timestamp. In Firefox, the difference was even bigger: about 250 to 350 times slower! Aha, so my hunch was right! Very gratifying. Then I took a step back. I had got caught up in a micro-optimization. Say we receive 100 messages/second, which can be considered a very busy feed. My benchmarking told me that 100 stop-starts of a timer takes about 6ms, so with 100 messages/second that equates to about 0.6% of one CPU core.

Conclusion: the simpler keep-alive processing is never going to be the bottleneck.

SSE Retry

SSE has its own stay-connected functionality. How does that work, and how does our code interact with it? The built-in reconnect of SSE is working at the socket level. If the socket is closed by the server, the browser will perform these steps:

- Set `readyState` (an element of our `EventSource` object) to CONNECTING.
- Call our `error` handler (see "Error Handling" on page 59).
- Wait `retry` seconds, and then connect again.

Who decides how long that retry delay is? The default is decided by your browser,[2] and is going to be about 3–5 seconds. What that means is that if the connection goes down due to a closed socket, the restart will happen before our keep-alive code gets a chance to notice. So there will not be any clash. The SSE restart will handle everything; our keep-alive restart will never be used.

Well, if SSE has this retry code built in, why did we bother writing our own keep-alive system? Good question. First, we will need it for the fallbacks that we will be looking at in the next two chapters. But even if we control the ecosystem and know all our browsers have `EventSource` support, we still need this code. The SSE reconnect only handles one of the things that can go wrong: the socket gets closed. There are other ways a data feed can stop working. Sockets can die in a way that is not noticed. The backend script could crash in a way that does not cleanly close the socket. It might enter an infinite loop. There could be a browser bug or a server bug. Luckily, our explicit keep-alive system takes care of all of these. But the most important one it takes care of is the case where the server is offline. When the web server cannot be reached, or sends back a 404, or is not configured for CORS correctly, SSE changes the `readyState` to CLOSED, and does not try again. Ever. Our explicit keep-alive system will retry every 20 seconds.

Going back to SSE retry, the default wait of 3–5 seconds is quite short. If your server is likely to close the connection a lot and does not want frequent reconnections, it can set the retry time higher. Conversely, if you want it shorter, to reduce downtime when

---

2. At the time of writing, it is 3 seconds in Chrome and Safari (see *core/page/EventSource.cpp* in the WebKit or Blink source code) and 5 seconds in Firefox (see *content/base/src/EventSource.cpp* in the Mozilla source code).

something goes wrong, you can set a lower number.[3] The way you do this is by sending a special SSE line:

```
retry: 10000
```

It is in milliseconds, so 10,000 means 10 seconds. I suggest you never set this higher than the rate at which you send keep-alives. For instance, if you set retry to 20000, then I suggest you have your server send keep-alives at 25- or 30-second intervals. (But don't go much higher than that or the browser and intermediaries, such as proxies, load balancers, etc., might start interpreting quietness as a lost connection.) And remember if you increase that interval on the server, you must increase keepaliveSecs in the JavaScript, too.

Perhaps we should take inspiration from the SSE retry, and implement our own protocol so that the server can also state the rate at which it is sending keep-alive messages, and we adjust keepaliveSecs automatically to match? It is a great idea for when the server is getting overloaded: dynamically tell clients to back off a bit. In reality, if you space the keep-alive messages out too far, the browser (or intermediaries) will think there is a problem, kill the socket, and will try to reconnect, thus creating more overall load. So you are only left with a range of about 15 to 40 seconds within which you can adjust. That makes little difference and is not worth the extra complexity involved.

In the book's source repository, there is a file called *fx_server.retry.php*. All it does is add one line at the top of the script, as shown here:

```
header("Content-Type: text/event-stream");

echo "retry: 10000\n\n";@flush();@ob_flush();

...
```

How do we test this? Well, the script contains a self-destruct clause! Just inside the top of the infinite loop, I've added this:

```
while(true){
  if(time() % 20) == 0)break;
  ...
```

At the start of each minute, and at 20 seconds past and 40 seconds past the start of each minute, the script will quietly exit. This is a nice clean exit, so the browser should learn about it immediately.

---

3. Firefox enforces a minimum reconnect time of 0.5 seconds.

Ways to Kill

Another way to test SSE recovery of a connection is to kill the server. For instance, if I'm using Apache on Ubuntu I can just type `sudo service apache2 restart`. As with breaking out of the infinite loop shown previously, this is a clean kill: the browser should recognize the socket has died almost immediately.

Incidentally, `sudo service apache2 graceful` is exactly what you don't want: it restarts all the Apache instances that are not doing anything, but your SSE process is doing something, so it keeps your SSE socket open.

What about ways to do a dirty kill?

If we run the server and client on different machines, we can simply pull out the network cable between them. Similarly, we could shut down the network interface on the server. The browser won't detect the socket has failed and our keep-alive process will get to do its work.

Another approach, when using Apache, is to work out which of the Apache processes is servicing our request, get its pid, then do `sudo kill -s STOP 12345`, where 12345 is the pid. This works like pulling out the cable: the browser won't detect the problem and instead our keep-alive will. The STOP signal means go to sleep. Use `sudo kill -s CONT 12345` to start it up again (equivalent to plugging the cable back in).

Why doesn't the browser detect the problem in the last two cases? Imagine if you pull out a cable for a second and then put it back in. Or you are connecting over mobile or WiFi and briefly go out of range, then come back in range again. By design, TCP/IP deals with these brief outages. The client cannot tell the difference between going quiet, a temporary problem, or a fatal problem. This is why we need a keep-alive system.

Point one of our client scripts at *fx_server.retry.php* to try it out. (*fx_client.retry.html* is supplied for this purpose; all that has changed is the URL to which it connects. Note that it has the keep-alive logic, so you can play with the interaction between the browser keep-alive and our own keep-alive.) With `retry:10000`, you will see 1–20 seconds of activity, then it will go quiet for 10 seconds. If you have the JavaScript console open, you will see an error appear: this is when the browser noticed that the socket disappeared. Then you will see it alternate between 10 seconds of activity (the seed of the new connection will be printed to screen) and 10 seconds of quiet. Try commenting out the retry header in *fx_server.retry.php*. With Firefox (which uses a 5-second default for `retry`), you will see 15 seconds of activity alternate with a 5-second quiet period. Now try setting the retry header to 500 (i.e., half a second), and you will see the errors appear in the console log, but almost no interruption of service.

Finally, try setting the retry to 21,000. This is higher than our own keep-alive check of 20 seconds. So our own code does the reconnect, not the browser SSE implementation. And now something fascinating happens: we end up connecting at 0, 20, and 40 seconds past each minute. This exactly matches the self-destruct times, and no data gets sent ever again! What fun. To be clear, this is just a chance interaction between the self-destruct time and the keep-alive timeout time. Try changing the self-destruct timing, or keepaliveSecs in your JavaScript, to get a feel for this. Or better still, keep retry to less than the keepaliveSecs and don't put self-destructs in your code. Ah, but, hang on, self-destruction is also the theme of the next section.

Adding Scheduled Shutdowns/Reconnects

In the real-world FX markets, there is no data to send on weekends.[4] All those sockets are being kept open, but all that is sent down them are keep-alive messages. Especially nowadays, with the cloud allowing us to change our computing capacity hour to hour, this is a waste. So what we want is for the server to be able to broadcast a message saying: "That's all folks. Tune in Monday morning for the next exciting episode."

On the backend, we could add this code:[5]

```
$when = strtotime("next Sunday 17:00 EST");
$until = date("Y-m-d H:i:s T", $when);
$untilSecs = time() - $when;
sendData( array(
  "action" => "scheduled_shutdown",
  "until" => $until,
  "until_secs" => $untilSecs
  ) );
```

This code sends the timestamp when the clients should reconnect, in the "until" field. We also send it as a Unix timestamp, the "until_secs" field, to make it easier for clients to work with. (It also means the client does not need to worry about differing time zones, or slow clocks: the server said come back in 100,000 seconds, so that is what we will do.)

Here we choose 5 p.m. Sunday afternoon, in EST (New York winter time), the traditional weekly start for FX trading. Our calculation of $until is a bit crude. If it is already Sunday, then "next Sunday" will go horribly wrong. Second, New York switches from EST (UTC-05) to EDT (UTC-04) for the summer. Or, in plainer language, we want to

---

4. We could have done this for the simulation server that was created in the earlier chapters: regularly look at the time and go to sleep for 48*3600 seconds at Friday, 5 p.m., New York time. But I left it as working 24/7 because chances are that you will want to try using the demo scripts on weekends. There is such a thing as too much realism!

5. Note: this assumes the script is running in the UTC (GMT) time zone. If your *server* is not set for UTC, then at the top of your PHP script use date_default_timezone_set('UTC');. Or if you write the timestamp you give to strtotime in the local server timestamp, it will work (but creates more work on the client).

---

use "EDT" from the second weekend in March through to the first weekend in November. PHP can do these calculations automatically for you, but that is starting to get outside the scope of this book. In a real application you will also want to consider public holidays, so you should consider getting all shutdown and reconnect times from a database rather than calculating them.

And in fact we will do something similar now (see *fx_server.shutdown.php*). The main loop now looks for the presence of a file on disk called *shutdown.txt*. It expects to find a datestamp in that file that strtotime can interpret.

 This is the first time we're using strtotime in the book; see "Date Handling" on page 199 in Appendix C if it is unfamiliar to you.

It will then send a shutdown to the clients, giving them that timestamp. This code has been added near the start of the main infinite loop:

```
$s = @file_get_contents("shutdown.txt");
if($s){
  $when = strtotime($s);
  $untilSecs = $when - time();
  if($when > 0 && $untilSecs > 0){
    $until = date("Y-m-d H:i:s T",$when);
    sendData( array(
      "action" => "scheduled_shutdown",
      "until" => $until,
      "until_secs" => $untilSecs
      ) );
    break;
    }
  }
```

The first line uses @ to suppress error messages. Effectively, it does a check for existence of the file, then loads it. If the file does not exist, $s will be false. The rest of the code is basically the example we saw earlier, with a bit of error-checking for bad timestamps (because we get it from a file that could contain anything).

So, because it is summertime as I write this, at Friday 5 p.m. EDT I will create a file with these contents: "next Sunday 17:00 EDT." I must make sure the file gets deleted by midnight on Saturday. (If I really didn't want clients connecting in the daytime on Sunday, I could replace it with a file that just read "17:00 EDT" for the first 17 hours of Sunday.)

Let's take a look at how we handle this on the frontend. There are two tasks: recognizing we got a shutdown message, and acting on it. For the first of those, we will add this to the end of our main loop:

```
...
else if(d.action=="scheduled_shutdown"){
  document.getElementById("msg").innerHTML +=
    "Scheduled shutdown from now. Come back at :" +
    d.until + "(in " + d.until_secs + " secs)<br/>";
  temporarilyDisconnect(d.until_secs);
  }
```

A first stab at the `temporarilyDisconnect()` function looks like this:

```
function temporarilyDisconnect(secs){
var millisecs = secs * 1000;
if(keepaliveTimer){
  clearTimeout(keepaliveTimer);
  keepaliveTimer = null;
  }
if(es){
  es.close();
  es = null;
  }
setTimeout(connect, millisecs);
}
```

Stop the keep-alive timer (we don't want that triggering while we're supposed to be sleeping!), close the SSE connection (when we add our fallbacks we need to put an entry in here for each to shut them down, too), and then call `connect()` at exactly the time we are told to.

I said "first stab," so you already know there is something wrong here…but it actually works perfectly. Test it (*fx_client.shutdown.html*). Start it running in your browser and then on the server, in the same directory as *fx_server.shutdown.php*, create a file called *shutdown.txt* and put a timestamp in that is about 30 seconds in the future. Use a 24-hour clock, and I recommend giving the time zone explicitly. For example, if you are in London, in summer, and it is currently 3:30:00 p.m., then try "15:30:30 BST" (remember how `strtime()` works; if you do not give a date, it defaults to the current day). It converts that to GMT, so in your browser you'll see a message something like "Scheduled shutdown from now. Come back at 2014-02-28 14:30:30 UTC(in 29 secs)." Wait those 29 seconds and it comes back to life. Just. Like. Magic.

It works perfectly. What on earth could be wrong? Here's a clue: it works *perfectly* and we call `connect()` at *exactly* the time we are told to. Have you spotted the hidden danger? Go back to the FX markets, and imagine you have 2,000 clients. Think what is going to happen on Sunday, at 17:00:00, New York time. They will all try to connect at that exact same moment and you have the mother of all traffic spikes.

How can we avoid this? An observation: it does not really matter if some clients come back a little earlier. So how about we add the couple of lines highlighted here:

```
function temporarilyDisconnect(secs){
var millisecs = secs * 1000;
millisecs -= Math.random() * 60000;
if(millisecs < 0)return;
if(keepaliveTimer){
  clearTimeout(keepaliveTimer);
  keepaliveTimer = null;
  }
if(es){
  es.close();
  es = null;
  }
setTimeout(connect, millisecs);
}
```

Try this out (*fx_client.jitter.html*). It randomly spreads the client connection attempts out over a 60-second period before the connect time we told them. The second line I added just says if that means there is no sleep needed at all, then don't even disconnect. By the way, you should delete *shutdown.txt* at least 60 seconds before the reconnect time. Otherwise, those early reconnecting clients just get told to go away again.

Sending Last-Event-ID

When we lose the connection and then reconnect, for whatever reason, we will get the new latest data when we reconnect. That is wonderful, but for any reasonably active data feed it means we will have a gap in our data. In Chapter 4 we went to the trouble of keeping a history of all the data we downloaded, but if it is not kept accurate and complete, it has much less value.

Fortunately, the designers of the SSE protocol gave this some thought. At connection time an HTTP header, Last-Event-ID, can be sent that specifies where the feed should start from. The ID is a string; it does not have to be a number.

The good news is that our fallbacks, using XMLHttpRequest and ActiveXObject, can use the setRequestHeader() function to simulate this behavior. The bad news is that we cannot specify it manually using EventSource. So with SSE we can only use the value that the server has previously sent to us, and *that* means that with a fresh connection we cannot specify it all. There is no setRequestHeader() function on the EventSource object (yet). This is one of those (rare) cases where our fallbacks are better than SSE.

> If you are thinking this restriction on not being able to send our own Last-Event-ID header must have to do with security, perhaps so the server can stop us from trying to access older data, I should point out you could get around it with any HTTP client library in any major computing language. Such security would be an illusion.

Imagine the case where we are reconnecting because our own keep-alive triggered. Or where the user has reloaded the page, and we are storing her history in an HTML5 LocalStorage object (therefore, we know the last data event she received, including its ID). For these cases, we will have to send the ID in the URL. So, the server has to look at both the URL and the Last-Event-ID header. The header should always get precedence (because that would mean it is one of the EventSource auto-reconnects, meaning the ID embedded in the URL is now out of date).

The next thing to consider is that there is only a single ID for a given SSE connection. If we are sending different data feeds (e.g., different FX exchange rates) down the same connection, what should we do? There is the easy way, and the hard way. The hard way is shown in the next section. The easy way, and the one we will use here, is to use the current time. Specifically, we will use the time on the server, and it will be in *milli*seconds since 1970. We use milliseconds since 1970 because that is the internal JavaScript format, so no conversion will be needed. How does it look on the server side? Just before each data line we send, we will send the time in the id field. So the client might receive a sequence of data like this:

```
id:1387946750885
data:{"symbol":"USD/JPY","timestamp":"2013-12-25 13:45:51",↵
  "rows":[{"id":1387946750112,"timestamp":"2013-12-25 13:45:50.112",↵
  "value":98.995},{"id":1387946750885,"timestamp":"2013-12-25 13:45:50.885",↵
  "value":98.980}]}

id:1387946751610
data:{"symbol":"USD/JPY","timestamp":"2013-12-25 13:45:51",↵
  "rows":[{"id":1387946751610,"timestamp":"2013-12-25 13:45:51.610",↵
  "value":98.985}]}
```

 The id: line can just as well come directly after the data: line, as long as both are before the blank line that marks the end of the SSE message.

Keen-eyed readers will notice that the data: lines have a different format than what we have been sending up to now. In each row we now send an id field, in addition to the timestamp. This is needed because in SSE (but ironically not in our fallbacks) we cannot get hold of the id row. Notice that the id is encoded in JSON as an integer, not a string.

I will start with the changes in the FXPair class. Relative to *fxpair.structured.php*, you will find just a couple of lines have changed in the generate() function of *fxpair.id.php*. The new version of generate() looks like this, with the additions highlighted:

```php
public function generate($t){
$bid = $this->bid;
$bid += $this->spread * 100 *
  sin( (360 / $this->long_cycle) *
  (deg2rad($t % $this->long_cycle)) );
$bid += $this->spread * 30 *
  sin( (360 / $this->short_cycle) *
  (deg2rad($t % $this->short_cycle)) );
$bid += (mt_rand(-1000,1000)/1000.0) * 10 * $this->spread;
$ask = $bid + $this->spread;

$ms = (int)($t * 1000);
$ts = gmdate("Y-m-d H:i:s",$t).sprintf(".%03d",$ms % 1000);
return array(
  "symbol" => $this->symbol,
  "timestamp" => $ts,
  "rows" => array(
    array(
      "id" => $ms,
      "timestamp" => $ts,
      "bid" => number_format($bid, $this->decimal_places),
      "ask" => number_format($ask, $this->decimal_places),
      )
    )
  );
}
```

$t is the number of seconds since 1970, with a fractional part. To get milliseconds since 1970, $ms, multiply by 1,000 (and because $t is to microsecond accuracy, then use (int) to truncate the microsecond part away). Sending this number back to the client is as easy as adding the 'id'=>$ms, line.

To have *fx_server.id.php* send the id back to SSE clients, just a couple of additions are needed relative to *fx_server.shutdown.php*. At the top, add include_once ("fxpair.id.php");, the new FXPair class. Then just below the definition of sendData(), add another helper function:

```php
function sendIdAndData($data){
$id = $data["rows"][0]["id"];
echo "id:".json_encode($id)."\n";
sendData($data);
}
```

So it outputs the id: row, then relies on sendData() to output the data: row and do the flush.

In the `sendIdAndData()` function just shown, we have this line: `echo "id:".json_encode($id)."\n";`. This could equally well have been `echo "id:$id\n";` because `$id` is an integer and therefore needs no special JSON encoding. Try changing it to see that the application behavior is identical. I've chosen to use `json_encode()` explicitly so that this code is ready to go if `$id` is a string or even something more complicated (see the following section).

Then in the middle of the main loop, change:

```
sendData( $symbols[$ix]->generate($t) );
```

into:

```
sendIdAndData( $symbols[$ix]->generate($t) );
```

To use it from the browser, just change the URL to connect to; there is nothing else to be done on the frontend, because SSE's use of `id:` is taken care of by the browser, behind the scenes.

Now that there is an integer ID in the row data, we could go back and change our history store to use that as the key, instead of the timestamp string. It should mean the key is 8 bytes instead of 24 bytes for the string. It might mean lookups are quicker. There is a catch, though: we also use that timestamp string in our interface. So either we still need to store it (more memory usage overall), or we need to make the timestamp from the milliseconds value, using JavaScript's `Date` functions (more CPU usage, though it does give us the flexibility to use different date formatting). I chose not to change anything.

Something to be careful of is that the ID should be the timestamp of the (most recent) data, *not* the current time. This is shown in the preceding code (I don't expect you to know the ID number, but the last three digits match the fraction of the second, and the fourth digit from the end is the last digit of the seconds). Of course, the timestamp on your new data and the current time are going to be close, but consider the case when the data being fed to the clients is coming to your server from another server, and to that server from another. The latency from all those hops could start to add up. We need to know the ID of the *data*, because when reconnecting, we use that ID to tell the server the last piece of *data* we saw, so that it can restart the feed from the very next item.

ID for Multiple Feeds

What if we have data feeds that are not being indexed by time? For instance, what if we are sending messages that we get by polling an SQL database, which uses an `autoin crement` primary key. Being given the timestamp in the `Last-Event-ID` header would require a search of the timestamp column, which is either slow or requires us to add another index column to our database (and that slows down database writes). What we really wanted in `Last-Event-ID` is the last value of the primary key that has been seen.

But then what if we are polling multiple tables? For instance, consider a chat application or a social network where we push out all kinds of notifications: chat messages, requests to chat, friends available for chat, friends who have logged off, new friend requests, etc. We need `Last-Event-ID` to tell us the latest ID seen in each of those tables.

Sounds hard, doesn't it? But I have some good news. The ID the server sends in the `id:` field, and that is sent back in `Last-Event-ID`, can be a string of any characters (to be precise, anything in Unicode except LF or CR). We settled on using JSON for the message we put in the `data:` lines, so why not do the same for the data we put in the `id:` line? It might look like this:

```
id:{"chatmessages":18304,"chatrequests":1048,"friendevents":8202}
```

The need to use this technique is not as contrived as it may sound. It is quite common in the finance industry to sell delayed data at a different price. For instance, a live feed of stock market share prices can be expensive, but Yahoo! and Google can show us 20-minute delayed prices for free. If you buy live data for just two symbols, and get the delayed prices for all the other symbols, your `lastId` variable is going to be continuously jumping back and forth 20 minutes. You are guaranteed that whatever its value when you need to do a reconnect, it is going to be wrong for some symbols. One solution is to send `id` like this:

```
id:{"live":1234123412,"delayed":1234123018}
```

One last thing to be careful of with using a JSON object for the `id:` field: if it gets past a hundred bytes or so, you cannot use GET, and will need to use cookies (See "HTTP POST with SSE" on page 139 in Chapter 9 to learn why HTTP POST is not a choice.) Then if it gets past a few thousand bytes, it is going to cause problems when sent as an HTTP header (remember SSE sends this header for you; you cannot control it). Specifically most web servers complain (send a 413 status code) if the total header size (request line, all headers, including the user agent and all cookies) exceeds 8KB.

Older versions of nginx have a 4KB limit, but the current default is 8KB, and it can be configured: *http://wiki.nginx.org/HttpCoreMod ule#large_client_header_buffers.* Apache can be similarly configured: *http://httpd.apache.org/docs/2.2/mod/core.html#limitrequest fieldsize.*

So, if your id: field is over a hundred bytes, stop and think if there is a better way. For instance, can the current position in each data source be stored server side, in a user session, and have that session referenced with a cookie?

Using Last-Event-ID

Back in the server-side script, how do we use the Last-Event-ID header? When using PHP, with Apache, headers sent by the browser get:

1. Changed to uppercase
2. Prefixed with HTTP_
3. Put in $_SERVER

In *fx_server.id.php*, here is what we do:

```
if(array_key_exists("HTTP_LAST_EVENT_ID", $_SERVER)){
    $lastId = $_SERVER["HTTP_LAST_EVENT_ID"];
    }
elseif(array_key_exists("lastId", $_POST)){
    $lastId = $_POST["lastId"];
    }
elseif(array_key_exists("lastId", $_GET)){
    $lastId = $_GET["lastId"];
    }
else $lastId = null;
```

(The lines mentioning $_POST and $_GET are explained in the next section.) Then I put the following code between setting $t based on finding seed in the HTTP request and using $t to set the random seed:

```
if($lastId)$t = $lastId / 1000.0;
```

In other words, because this is only a test application, I'm basically using the Last-Event-ID header as a synonym for seed. For the sake of testing and understanding how Last-Event-ID works, this is good enough; in a real application, this is where you would do the history request, then send a patch of the missing data.

Security Alert! `lastId` is pure, unadulterated user input. It can theoretically contain anything; never assume it will only ever contain what your frontend JavaScript puts in it. A hacker could put whatever he wants in it.

The preceding code is actually secure, but in this case the security check is very subtle: I expect `$lastId` to be a number. When I divide by `1000.0`, if it is anything but a number, PHP will first implicitly convert it to a number. If a hacker has set `lastId` to be `{"hello":"tell me your password"}`, that ends up as `0` before being divided by `1000.0`. `$t` gets set to January 1, 1970. The worst thing that a hacker can do is put `$t` as a date in the far past or far future.

When `lastId` contains other types of data, you have more work to do to sanitize it and understand the potential risks. This isn't a book on web security, so I suggest you read up on the sanitization techniques available for the backend language you are using.

How to test? The same way we tested the `retry:` header earlier (see "Ways to Kill" on page 67). So, try cutting the connection (have your JavaScript console open so you can see when the disappearance of the SSE socket is noticed by the browser) and after a few seconds the browser reconnects and continues with the quotes from the timestamp it had reached.

You will notice the quotes start falling behind the wall clock! This is just a side effect of it being artificial test data. If it really bothers you, find a good therapist.

Getting Last-Event-ID in Node.js

The code shown in this section was using some features quite specific to PHP, so how does it look in Node.js? The following example has been grafted onto *basic_sse_node_servers.js*, which we saw back in Chapter 2:

```
var url = require("url");
...
http.createServer(function(request, response){
  var urlParts = url.parse(request.url, true);
  if(urlParts.pathname != "/sse"){
    ...
  }

  var lastId = null;
  if(request.headers["last-event-id"]){
    lastId = request.headers["last-event-id"];
```

```
        }
    else if(urlParts.query["lastId"])lastId = urlParts.query["lastId"];
    console.log("Last-Event-ID:" + lastId);

    //The SSE data is streamed here

    }).listen(port);
```

(You can find this code as *basic_sse_node_server.headers.js* in the book's source code.)

HTTP headers are found in `request.headers`. Nice and easy. Just remember they have been lowercased.

To get the GET data requires parsing `request.url`, which is done at the top of the function. After that, the GET data can be found in `urlParts.query`.

You notice I do not show how to get POST data. It is a bit more involved, though only to the tune of six lines or so.[6] But the real complication is that the parsing is asynchronous. So the code would need to be refactored to use callbacks, which is getting a bit involved for this sidebar!

Passing the ID at Reconnection Time

During the previous section I showed how to get `$lastId` from the `Last-Event-ID` header. But I also included code to look in the POST and GET data for a variable named `lastId`. This allows us to specify the ID ourselves on a fresh connection, not rely on the underlying SSE protocol. Why do we need this? Because `EventSource` currently has no way to allow us to send our own HTTP headers. No, but *why* do we need this? It is needed in two cases:

- When our keep-alive has triggered and it is our JavaScript doing the reconnect, not the browser's implementation of SSE
- When reloading the page in the browser, and a cookie or `LocalStorage` object knows the last ID we've seen

Take note of the order of the code: it is first come, first served. If the header is present, then that is used. Otherwise, we look in the POST data (this is actually for the fallbacks in the next two chapters; native SSE does not support POST-ing data). If neither the `Last-Event-ID` header nor `lastId` is in the POST data, then and only then will it look for `lastId` in the URL. This is important because when SSE sends the `Last-Event-ID` header to reconnect it will be using the same URL. If we let the GET data have precedence over the `Last-Event-ID` header, it will be using an old ID and not the latest one.

---

6. You can find a good discussion of this at *http://stackoverflow.com/q/4295782/841830*.

Over on the client side, what changes do we need to make? Start with a global:

```
var lastId = null;
```

If you are saving permanent state in a LocalStorage object, you would initialize lastId from that.

We only want lastId pasted into the URL for SSE, not for the other fallbacks (because we can set HTTP headers for them). So instead of connect(), we change startEvent Source(), which currently looks like this:

```
function startEventSource(){
if(es)es.close();
es = new EventSource(url);
es.addEventListener("message",
  function(e){processOneLine(e.data);}, false);
es.addEventListener("error", handleError, false);
}
```

to the following (changes in bold):

```
function startEventSource(){
if(es)es.close();
var u = url;
if(lastId)u += "lastId="
  + encodeURIComponent(lastId) + "&";
es = new EventSource(u);
es.addEventListener("message",
  function(e){processOneLine(e.data);}, false);
es.addEventListener("error", handleError, false);
}
```

The last step is where the refactoring in Chapter 4 (adding an id field to each row of data) can finally bear fruit. In function processOneLine(s), there is currently this loop:

```
for(var ix in d.rows){
  var r = d.rows[ix];
  x.innerHTML = d.rows[ix].bid;
  full_history[d.symbol][r.timestamp] = [r.bid, r.ask];
  }
```

Now add one line to the end of the loop, so that the lastId global always contains the highest ID received so far:

```
for(var ix in d.rows){
  var r = d.rows[ix];
  x.innerHTML = d.rows[ix].bid;
  full_history[d.symbol][r.timestamp] = [r.bid, r.ask];
  lastId = r.id;
  }
```

Again, if using Web Storage to persist data even after the browser is shut, you would update that here (e.g., localStorage.lastId = r.id;) too.

IDs and Multiple Upstream Data Sources

Remember that the approach described in the main text (a single global for `lastId`) only works when all symbols (aka multiplexed data feeds) share the same ID system. In our case, all the symbols use `id` to mean the time of the quote (in milliseconds since 1970).

But even when using a timestamp as the unique ID, there is need for care. If the system is broadcasting share prices from two or more exchanges, then those two exchanges could be slightly out of sync, or one might have experienced a temporary delay. As an example, you have received prices up to 14:30:27.450 for the New York Stock Exchange, but the last NASDAQ price seen was 14:30:22.120 and 5 seconds' worth of prices are currently delayed, and then you lost your own connection. When you reconnect, if you say the last price seen was at 14:30:27.450, you would miss out on those 5 seconds of NASDAQ prices. If instead you request prices since 14:30:22.120, you get 5 seconds of duplicate NYSE information.

So when dealing with two upstream data sources, maintain the last ID for each (see "ID for Multiple Feeds" on page 75).

To test this we need to force a keep-alive timer to timeout, meaning that our script has to go quiet, but not die (if the socket dies cleanly, the SSE reconnect will kick in first). One way to do that is to put the following code at the top of our infinite main loop over in *fx_server.id.php* :

```
if($t % 10 == 0){sleep(45);break;}
```

In other words, go to sleep for a long time and then exit, every 10 seconds. (The client will have disconnected before `sleep()` returns, causing the PHP process to be shut down so the `break` is not really needed.) If you use that method, it will hit a problem when it reconnects, because `$t` will be divisible by 10, so it will immediately fail. Ad infinitum. A workaround for that is to place this line just before entering the infinite main loop. It just fast-forwards the clock to get past the divisible-by-10 point:

```
while($t % 10 == 0 || $t % 10 == 9)$t += 0.25;
```

 If you want a ready-made version, see *fx_server.die_slowly.php* in the book's source code, which is paired with *fx_client.die_slowly.html* (the only change from *fx_client.id.html* is the URL it connects to).

When you test this, you should see a few seconds of quotes come through. Then it stops. After 20 seconds (the keep-alive timer length), it connects again and you should see quotes pick up from where it left off. (See "Ways to Kill" on page 67 for ways to dirty-kill a socket so you can test how this code copes with that.)

Don't Act Globally, Think Locally

Up until now all our code has used a bunch of global variables. Appendix B explains why this is bad, and what we can do about it, but the bottom line is that using those globals is stopping code reuse: we cannot have more than one SSE connection on a page. The following listing is based on *fx_client.id.html*, but adds the highlighted sections:

```
var url = "fx_server.id.php?";

function SSE(url,options){
if(!options)options={};
var defaultOptions={
  keepaliveSecs: 20
  };
for(var key in defaultOptions)
  if(!options.hasOwnProperty(key))
    options[key]=defaultOptions[key];

var es = null;
var fullHistory = {};
var keepaliveTimer = null;
var lastId = null;

function gotActivity(){
if(keepaliveTimer != null)
  clearTimeout(keepaliveTimer);
keepaliveTimer = setTimeout(
  connect, options.keepaliveSecs * 1000);
}
.
. (all other functions untouched)
.
connect();
}

setTimeout(function(){new SSE(url);}, 100);
```

There are two main changes:

- Encapsulate all the variables and functions, so that SSE is the only thing in the global scope, and multiple instances could be created.

- Introduce an options parameter, where everything is optional. keepaliveSecs was moved in here.

I said multiple instances *could* be created, but it would be silly to just create two instances here without thinking about your data and how it is to be displayed. Currently, the code is hardwired to use the static HTML found in *fx_client.closure.html*. So two instances would end up competing for control of the HTML. What to do? If you want a single HTML table to show merged data from two data feeds (e.g., USD/JPY comes from one feed, EUR/USD comes from another feed) then `fullHistory` should be pulled out of the `SSE` constructor and returned to being a global, along with `updateHistoryTable()` and `makeHistoryTbody()`. On the other hand, if you want two sets of data to appear in the browser, you should wrap each block of HTML in a div, and give the ID of that div as a parameter to the SSE object. (See "Tea for Two, and Two for Tea" on page 193 for an example of the latter approach.)

Cache Prevention

The browser would be silly to cache streaming data. However, it never hurts to get a bit explicit. So, near the top of your script (near where you set the `Content-Type` header), add these lines:

```
header("Cache-Control: no-cache, must-revalidate");
header("Expires: Sun, 31 Dec 2000 05:00:00 GMT");
```

The first one is for HTTP/1.1, and should really be the only thing you need, given that HTTP/1.1 was defined in 1999. But there are still some old proxies around, so that is what the second line is for; it just has to be any date in the past. You could also add `header('Pragma: no-cache');` as a third line, but it should be completely redundant in both old and new browsers, servers, and proxies.

Death Prevention

This code is PHP-specific, and is more important on Windows than Linux; if your script keeps dying after 30 seconds, this might well be the fix. I've left the explanation of why to "Falling Asleep" on page 200. Just throw this line at the top of your script (right after the `date_default_timezone_set('UTC');` line is just perfect):

```
set_time_limit(0);
```

The Easy Way to Lose Weight

Shed those pounds the easy way! Just take this tasty pill and watch your dreams come true:

```
AddOutputFilterByType DEFLATE text/html text/plain text/xml text/event-stream
```

If inserted in the correct place (i.e., your Apache server configuration), this will run gzip compression on the data sent back. But first look for a line similar to that in your existing configuration; perhaps you just need to add `text/event-stream` to the list. For instance, in Ubuntu there is a file called *deflate.conf* (under */etc/apache2/mods-enabled/*) and I added `text/event-stream` to the end of the line that mentions `text/plain`.

Another way to configure Apache is to `DEFLATE` everything except a few image formats. That might look like this (and if this is what you already use, there is nothing to add for SSE):

```
<Location />
  SetOutputFilter DEFLATE
  SetEnvIfNoCase Request_URI \.(?:gif|jpe?g|png)$ no-gzip dont-vary
  Header append Vary User-Agent env=!dont-vary
</Location>
```

Learn more about Apache configuration of compression at *http://httpd.apache.org/docs/2.4/mod/mod_deflate.html*. The `Vary` header is added to avoid some issues with proxies.

If using IIS as your web server, this article explains how to configure compression for dynamic content: *http://technet.microsoft.com/en-us/library/cc753681.aspx*.

If using nginx, see *http://nginx.org/en/docs/http/ngx_http_gzip_module.html*. Note that you might want `gzip_min_length` to be set to 0, or some low number, to make sure it works for streaming content, too.

Looking Back

In this chapter we have tried to improve the *quality* of our application, by reporting errors, sending keep-alives, avoiding caching problems, and reconnecting when there is a problem. For reconnecting we use both SSE's built-in `retry` mechanism, and our own, both relying on the application sending us an ID number that tells us the latest data seen so far. We also looked at scheduled shutdowns and supporting multiple connections.

The next couple of chapters work on the *coverage* of this application, instead of the quality, allowing browsers without SSE support to receive the same data while keeping all the production-quality features introduced here.

CHAPTER 6

Fallbacks: Data Push for Everyone Else

What we are going to look at in this chapter is a fallback approach, called *long-polling*, that (with a few tweaks) works just about everywhere. If the data being pushed is relatively infrequent, its inefficiency won't even be noticed and you could get away with using it everywhere, but generally we will just use it for browsers where there is no native SSE support.

In both this and the next chapter I will start by showing the code in a minimal example. Then, after that, the FX demo from the end of Chapter 5 will be adapted to work with long poll. By the end of this chapter we will have 99% coverage (albeit with varying levels of inefficiency) for our production-quality, realistic, data push application.

Browser Wars

The differences between browsers (aka "The Browser Wars") have been annoying us since the mid-1990s, but they became especially troublesome when Microsoft threw its hat into the ring and we went through a phase where each browser manufacturer tried to make the Web better, unilaterally, attempting to differentiate its product with *features*. That wasn't what either the end users (you and me) or the content developers (again, you and me) wanted. Standards got discussed and ignored; it is only in the past few years that all the browser manufacturers have started taking standards seriously. The browser manufacturers finally realized they should differentiate themselves on user interface and speed, not proprietary features.

But we still have their mess to deal with. And when it comes to using the latest HTML5 technologies, the mess is still being created and it is going to be around for the next 3–4 years, at least. When it comes to SSE I am going to shine the spotlight of shame first on Google, then Microsoft. The built-in Android browser only started supporting SSE as of Android 4.4 (though many earlier Android devices use Chrome, which does support SSE); the XHR fallback (described in the next chapter) works since Android 3, but fails on Android 2.x (which still has a large number of users at the time of writing; see *http://bit.ly/wiki-android-versions*).

Over in the blue corner, Microsoft has made Internet Explorer (IE) more standards-compliant with each release, so much so that IE9 and later get grudging approval from most web developers. But, as of IE11, SSE is not supported, and next chapter's XHR fallback does not work on IE9 and earlier. There is another fallback, iframe, also covered in Chapter 7, that only works on IE8 and above.

The long-poll approach shown in this chapter is not quite as efficient as native SSE (or the fallbacks we will study in Chapter 7), but for Android 2.x and IE6/7, it is the only choice. Actually, the inefficiency won't be noticed in most applications. But if you are sending multiple updates per second, it is possible that the extra resource usage (client-side CPU, server-side CPU, and network bandwidth) will become noticeable.

 That is not to say you cannot use long-poll at subsecond frequencies. I've tested it at 10 updates/second, with no degradation. At 100 updates/second, and passing an ID to specify the last received data (see "Sending Last-Event-ID" on page 71), it keeps up—you get all the data, but it comes through in lumps: you won't get 100 distinct messages each second.

What Is Polling?

Before I tell you what *long-polling* is, we should first talk about regular polling, which is shown graphically in Figure 6-1. Regular polling is where you knock on the door of your best friend and ask "Are you ready to play?" and she immediately says "yes" or "no." If she says "yes," you go out and have fun. If she says "no," she shuts the door in your face, and 30 seconds later you knock on the door and ask her (poll her) again. Eventually she'll be ready. Or she was only pretending to be your best friend. Or you had garlic for breakfast.

The really odd thing that I want you to understand about regular polling is that once your friend is finally ready, she will just sit there, staring at the wall like a zombie, waiting for you to come and knock on the door again.

In the context of our FX demo, regular polling means that at a fixed rate, say every 10 seconds, we do an Ajax HTTP request to ask for data. When we do regular polling we have to decide if we want to do *sampling* or if we want to receive *everything*. If we are sampling, the server will send the latest price for all symbols. Just one price for each symbol. The client will get price snapshots, but not the prices between each of the polling requests. The alternative to sampling is that each time we poll the server we also send the timestamp of the last update we received, and request all updates since that time. The backend server might reply with a blank array to say no updates, or it might reply

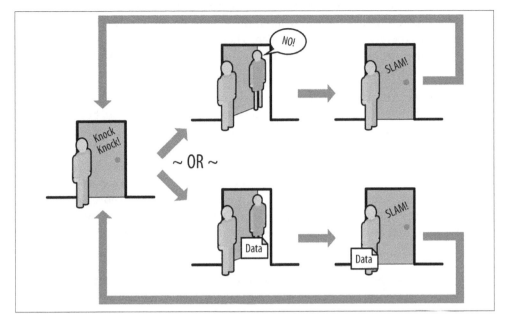

Figure 6-1. Polling your friend

with a huge array if there have been lots of updates. Compared to sampling, you are able to maintain a full history on the client side.

How Does Long-Polling Work?

So, how is long-polling different from regular polling? Going back to our best friend, we go and knock on her door, and say, "Are you ready to play?" and she replies, "No, but let's leave the door open and as soon as I'm ready I will come and tell you." See Figure 6-2 and notice how you only knock on the door once, how the door stays open, and how *each and every* visit gets data.

Figure 6-2. Long-polling your friend

In the context of our FX demo, we do the Ajax HTTP request, but we don't ask for the latest price. Instead we ask to be told about the next price change. If things have gone quiet, it just sits there, holding a socket open. Then as soon as the price changes, it sends it, and shuts the socket. We then *immediately* make another long-poll connection, for the next price change.

The key difference between SSE and long-poll is we need a new HTTP connection for each piece of data. We still have the downside that SSE/WebSocket had, because we are using up a dedicated socket practically all the time. Latency-wise, it is almost as good as SSE: when a new price arrives we get to hear about it immediately. It's almost but not quite as good, because making the new HTTP connection each time takes a few milliseconds. And once you turn up the rate of messages to 10 or more per second, that "just a few milliseconds" for each new connection starts to take up the majority of the time. (On slow latency networks such as mobile, that few milliseconds might actually be hundreds or even thousands of milliseconds, so it's slow right from the start.)

Is Long-Polling Always Better Than Regular Polling?

Which is best depends on your definition of *better*. From the point of view of latency, long-polling is always better: as soon as the server has a new value, you get it. In regular polling you have to wait until the next time you poll to discover it. (This latency advantage also applies to SSE and the other fallbacks we discuss in the next chapter.)

But what about from the point of view of overall bandwidth usage? The answer to that is not so clear cut. If your FX prices update twice a second, long-polling has to make 120 HTTP requests each minute. If you were instead doing regular polling once every 10 seconds, you only had to make six HTTP requests each minute. So regular polling is better. But, conversely, if your FX prices update twice a minute, with long-polling you only had to make two HTTP requests each minute, whereas regular polling every 10 seconds still had to make six HTTP requests. And latency is still worse!

Knowledge of your data, and exactly when it will update, can also be used with long-poll or native SSE: disconnect when not expecting any data. This gives you the same latency (assuming you reconnect in time), but saves on socket usage (and associated costs like an Apache process). This was the technique we showed in "Adding Scheduled Shutdowns/Reconnects" on page 68. (If you end up using it, pay close attention to why the reconnects were randomly jittered.)

Show Me Some Code!

That was a lot of words, so how about some code, for balance? First, the backend:

```php
<?php
usleep(2500000); //2.5s
header("Content-Type: text/plain");
echo date("Y-m-d H:i:s")."\n";
```

Short and simple. Save this as *minimal_longpoll.php* and put it on your web server. When you call it, there is a 2.5 second wait and then it shows you the current timestamp. About the only thing I need to point out about the code is that we send the header *after* the sleep, not before. The sleep is simulating waiting for our next piece of data, and until we get that data we will not know what kind of data we are sending. For instance, we might end up needing to send back an error code instead, based on some external event, in which case the code would be something like this:

```php
<?php
usleep(2500000); //2.5s
$cat = (rand(1,2) == 1) ? "dead" : "alive";
if($cat == "dead"){
    header("HTTP/1.0 404 Not Found");
    echo "Something bad happened. Sorry.";
    }else{
    header("Content-Type: text/plain");
    echo date("Y-m-d H:i:s")."\n";
    }
```

Now for the frontend. Put *minimal_longpoll_test.html* in the same directory as *mini mal_longpoll.php*, and try loading it in a browser. You will see "Preparing!" flash on screen for a moment, then the JavaScript runs and it gets replaced by "Started!" Then a moment later it gets replaced with .[1]. This tells you a connection has been made (readyState==1). Two and a half seconds later it will typically show .[1].[2].[3]. [4] followed by the timestamp, then on the next line another .[1] (meaning another long-poll connection has been made). What you see might vary from browser to browser, depending on exactly how Ajax has been implemented; it is only the [1] (Ajax request started) and the [4] (Ajax request completed) that are important. See "Ajax ready-State" on page 91 to learn what the 1, 2, 3, and 4 mean.

```html
<!DOCTYPE html>
<html>
  <head>
    <noscript>
      <meta http-equiv="refresh"
                content="0;URL=longpoll.nojs.php">
    </noscript>
    <meta charset="utf-8" />
    <title>Minimal long-poll test</title>
  </head>
  <body>
    <p id="x">Preparing!</p>
    <script>
    function onreadystatechange(){
        s += ".[" + this.readyState + "]";
```

```
        document.getElementById('x').innerHTML = s;
        if(this.readyState != 4)return;
        s += this.responseText + "<br/>\n";
        document.getElementById('x').innerHTML = s;
        setTimeout(start, 50);
        }

    function start(){
        var xhr;
        if(window.XMLHttpRequest){
           xhr = new XMLHttpRequest();
           }
        else{
           xhr = new ActiveXObject("Msxml2.XMLHTTP");
           }
        xhr.onreadystatechange = onreadystatechange;
        xhr.open('GET', 'minimal_longpoll.php?t=' +
           (new Date().getTime()));
        xhr.send(null);
        }

    var s = "";
    setTimeout(start,100);
    document.getElementById('x').innerHTML = "Started!";
    </script>

  </body>
</html>
```

Start your study of the source code by looking at the `start()` function. This initiates a long-poll request. First we create our `XMLHttpRequest` object, unless we are on Internet Explorer, in which case we create an `Msxml2.XMLHTTP` ActiveX object. The two objects have the same functions and behavior, so all other code is the same. The next line, `xhr.onreadystatechange = onreadystatechange;`, tells it the name of the callback function we want all data to be sent to. As an aside, we could have used JQuery to hide this Ajax complexity. But there isn't that much complexity in the end, just two or three extra lines.

Then we do `xhr.open` to say which page to get data from, and `xhr.send()` to actually start everything going. (The explicit null parameter to `send()` is needed on some browsers.)

At the beginning of this chapter, I mentioned that a few tweaks were needed to get long-poll working in all browsers. The first of those is that some browsers (e.g., Android) will cache the Ajax request. To avoid this, we append something to the URL. A simple approach is to use the current timestamp, expressed as milliseconds since 1970.

With IE6/7 there is another thing we need to be careful of: we must use a fresh XHR object for each request. If, instead, we create the XHR object once, then just call `send()` again each time we want to start a long-poll request, it works in all browsers *except*

Internet Explorer 7 and earlier. But by creating a fresh object each time, it works everywhere. We do it that way for all browsers; it is not really any extra trouble.

Another tweak is the very first call to start(). Instead of calling it directly, we use setTimeout to add a 100ms delay. This is needed by some versions of Safari, at least. Without it, you see a permanent loading spinner. There has to be enough time for the rest of the page to be parsed and made ready. (It is not needed by Android, in my testing, so if Android is the only one of your supported browsers using long-poll, you could try removing the 100ms delay.)

The next function I would like you to look at is onreadystatechange ("on-ready-state-change"). This is a callback function that is called as it progresses through the request; see the following sidebar. All we are interested in here is when readyState becomes 4, because that means we've received some new data. It also means the remote server has closed the connection.

Ajax readyState

An XMLHttpRequest object (and also Internet Explorer's Msxml2.XMLHTTP ActiveX object) can be in a number of different states. You don't normally need to care, and if you have only ever made your Ajax connections using jQuery, you won't even have met them. The states are a number from 0 to 4, with the following meanings:

0

Request has not started yet.

1

A connection to the server has been made.

2

The request (and any post data) has been sent to the server.

3

Getting data.

4

Got all data and connection has closed.

For long-poll (and short-poll, and normal Ajax usage), we ignore everything we get until readyState becomes 4. Our onreadystatechange callback is called exactly once for when readyState is 4. In the next chapter we will look at a technique where we do care about readyState 3. It might be called more than once. Different browsers treat it differently, and some make the data loaded so far available, while others do not. Different browsers treat readyState 0, 1, and 2 differently, so you cannot always rely on them being given to you.

So, we output a period each time the function is called, but if `readyState` is not yet 4, then that is all we do. Once `readyState` has become 4, we output the message the server has sent us (found in `responseText`), and then we initiate the next long-poll request by calling `start()`.

There is a 50ms delay on calling `start()`, again done with `setTimeout()` because otherwise some browsers get confused and eventually complain about stack overflows and such. Long-poll is our fallback for the dumbest browsers, so don't sweat having to introduce a bit of extra latency. (Again, Android does not appear to need the 50ms delay in my testing.)

Optimizing Long-Poll

I mentioned earlier that long-poll is fine most of the time, but starts to become quite inefficient when things heat up. If we are sending a new update twice every second, that is up to 120 new HTTP requests a minute that have to be made. When this happens, there are two things we can do to reduce the load a bit.

The first is easy: have the client go slower. In fact, our code already does this—we have a 50ms sleep before initiating the next long-poll request. If you increased that from 50 to 1000, then the absolute maximum number of long-poll requests we can make is 60 per minute. Allowing for some network overhead, you are looking at a maximum of 40 to 50 requests per minute. When data is less frequent, the extra delay causes no real problem: you get your next update after 16 seconds instead of 15 seconds. You can think of the length of that sleep as the continuum between the extremes of long-poll (zero latency, possibly lots of requests) and regular-poll (predictable latency, predictable request rate).

The other approach is server side. We could buffer up data for the long-poll clients, sending their data no more than once/second. How would this work? First, make a note of the time they connect (for example, 18:30:00.000). Then, say, we have data available to send to clients at 18:30:00.150, but we decide not to flush the data yet, because it has been less than a second since they connected. So instead we hold on to it, and set a timeout of 850ms. But before that timer triggers (at, for example, 18:30:00.900), we get more data to send to clients. Still we wait—another 100ms. No new data arrives in those 100ms so now we flush it and close the connection. The client gets two data items together.

Alternatively, how about if the client connects at 18:30:00.000, but the first new data comes through at 18:30:01.100 (1.1 seconds after the request started)? In that case we send it immediately and close the connection. In other words, the artificial latency is only being introduced when multiple messages come through in the space of a single second, which effectively means we only slow things down when there are a lot of messages. This is just what we want.

I suggest that if you do this, you have the minimum time easily customizable, so that you can easily experiment with values between 500 and 2000 milliseconds.

What If JavaScript Is Disabled?

If JavaScript is disabled, then nothing described in this chapter works. When the user runs our minimal example, they will see "Preparing!" on screen for the rest of their natural lives. And it is nothing more than they deserve. Nothing described in any of the other chapters works either.

What's that? You sympathize with them? Bah, humbug. But, yes, there is a way to send updates to these 20th-century-ers. We're going to just modify the *minimal_longpoll_ex ample.html* files, not the fuller FX price demo. First, add this immediately after the <head> tag:

```
<noscript>
  <meta http-equiv="refresh" content="0;URL=longpoll.nojs.php">
</noscript>
```

Because it is between the <noscript> tags, it does nothing for almost everyone. But, what it does is send our JavaScript-disabled users to another page. That other page is PHP, not HTML. That PHP script has to generate a full HTML page, not just send the data, as it can when called over Ajax. The code is quite straightforward:

```
<!DOCTYPE html>
<html>
  <head>
    <script>window.location.href="minimal_longpoll_test.html"</script>
    <meta http-equiv="refresh" content="3">
    <meta charset="utf-8" />
    <title>Update test when JS disabled</title>
  <head>
  <body>
    <p><?= date("Y-m-d H:i:s"); ?></p>
    <p>(Enable JavaScript for better responsiveness.)</p>
  </body>
</html>
```

The key line is <meta http-equiv="refresh" content="3">, which says "reload this page after 3 seconds." After 3 seconds an HTTP request is made, and the PHP script will run again and create a new web page, with a new timestamp in it.

I'd also like to point out the <script> line at the top of that file. This is a clever little trick: if the users had just temporarily disabled JavaScript, then as soon they enable JavaScript, it will be detected on the very next page refresh and will take them back to your full-service live-updating site, where they will be welcomed to the 21st century with open arms.

Grafting Long-Poll onto Our FX Application

At the end of Chapter 5, we finished with a fairly robust demo application. It generates random FX data, with multiple symbols (multiplexing) and multifield data. It can maintain a history of all data received, and do interesting things with that history, such as charts and tables. It reconnects when things go wrong, and keeps track of the point up to which it's seen data, as well as scheduled shutdowns and reconnects.

Luckily, to graft long-poll on to that existing application is not too much work. Did I just say *luckily*? In fact, the ease with which we can graft on an alternative delivery method is a direct result of all the little design decisions that were made in the previous few chapters.

Connecting

The FX application currently has an SSE object with a private variable called es and a function called startEventSource(). Our first task is to create the equivalent for long-poll.[1] Here are the new private variables added to the SSE object:

```
var xhr = null;
var longPollTimer = null;
```

As you can see, there is also a variable to store the timer handle (this is only used by disconnect()). And here are the functions we need to add:

```
function startLongPoll(){
if(window.XMLHttpRequest)xhr = new XMLHttpRequest();
else xhr = new ActiveXObject("Msxml2.XMLHTTP");
xhr.onreadystatechange = longPollOnReadyStateChange;
var u = url;
u += "longpoll=1&t=" + (new Date().getTime());
xhr.open("GET", u);
if(last_id)xhr.setRequestHeader("Last-Event-ID", last_id);
xhr.send(null);
}

function longPollOnReadyStateChange(){
if(this.readyState != 4)return;
longPollTimer = setTimeout(startLongPoll, 50);
processNonSSE(this.responseText);
}
```

The startLongPoll() function and its onreadystatechange callback are basically the same functions we saw earlier in this chapter, but with a few small differences:

---

1. The es and xhr variables are exclusive. In other words, either a browser will use es and xhr will always be null, or it will use xhr and es will always be null. So they could share the same variable name, perhaps called server. I have chosen not to, to emphasize that each holds a different type of JavaScript object. Another reason to use different names is for when closing them: es.close() but xhr.abort().

- Use the `url` global, instead of hardcoding the URL to connect to.

- Pass the `Last-Event-ID` header, when `last_id` is set. See "Sending Last-Event-ID" on page 71. Unlike with `EventSource`, it is possible to send HTTP headers with `XMLHttpRequest` (and with Internet Explorer's `ActiveXObject` too), and so we do.

- The processing is handed to `processNonSSE()`, which will be written shortly.

- `longpoll=1` is added to the URL. This is so the backend knows to disconnect after sending data. (Remember, with long-poll the data does not get seen by the browser until the connection is closed.) By using this, we can have a single backend servicing the various frontend fallbacks.

- The timer handle is recorded, so the timer can be cancelled by other code.

One more small addition is needed. In `temporarilyDisconnect()` there are a couple of tidy-up tasks:

```
if(keepaliveTimer != null)clearTimeout(keepaliveTimer);
if(es)es.close();
```

We could just add `if(xhr)xhr.abort();`, but there will be more to do in the next chapter, so let's move all three commands to a `disconnect()` function, and call that from `temporarilyDisconnect()`. So the two functions look like this:

```
function disconnect(){
if(keepaliveTimer){
  clearTimeout(keepaliveTimer);
  keepaliveTimer = null;
  }
if(es){
  es.close();
  es = null;
  }
if(xhr){
  xhr.abort();
  xhr = null;
  }
if(longPollTimer){
  clearTimeout(longPollTimer);
  longPollTimer = null;
  }
}

function temporarilyDisconnect(secs){
var millisecs = secs * 1000;
millisecs -= Math.random() * 60000;
if(millisecs < 0)return;
disconnect();
setTimeout(connect,millisecs);
}
```

Long-Poll and Keep-Alive

If you remember back to the section "Client Side" on page 62, you know our keep-alive system is set up to call `connect()` if we don't get any activity on the connection after 20 seconds. This causes a problem for long-poll because there is no way for long-poll to send keep-alives: it sends one message and disconnects. Well, of course, the server will happily *send* the keep-alives, but our client won't receive them.

In those browsers where `onreadystatechanged` gets called for `ready State==3` messages, we can get those keep-alives. But, if we can do *that*, then we would be using the XHR technique described in the next chapter, not bothering with the current long-poll technique.

See the *longpoll_keepalive.php* and *longpoll_keepalive.html* files in the book's source code if you want to play around with this. It sends keep-alives every 2 seconds, then sends the real data after 10 seconds and exits. See what you get, and when, in each browser. In Android 2.3 (the main need for long-poll, if you support mobile users), you will see the callback is called immediately for `readyState==1`, but then there is nothing for 10 seconds and states 2, 3, and 4 all come through together at the end.

So, if our long-poll does not send anything within 20 seconds, what happens? Something not good. `startLongPoll` gets called again, so now we have two sockets open to the server. If the server doesn't send anything for hours we will have hundreds of sockets open. Really? Hundreds? Kind of. Remember that if the server is sending keep-alives, the sockets will all be active, and so won't be getting killed off. But not hundreds, because browsers have a limit on the number of simultaneous connections, typically six. In a sense this is worse: after a short time there will be six long-poll connections open, new requests will quietly get put on a stack, and all other communication with that server (e.g., for new images) will also be put on hold.

By adding the following two highlighted lines, we can avoid this Armageddon scenario:

```
function startLongPoll(){
if(xhr)xhr.abort();
if(window.XMLHttpRequest)xhr = new XMLHttpRequest();
else xhr = new ActiveXObject("Msxml2.XMLHTTP");
xhr.onreadystatechange = longPollOnReadyStateChange;
var u = url;
u += "longpoll=1&t=" + (new Date().getTime());
xhr.open("GET", u);
if(lastId)xhr.setRequestHeader("Last-Event-ID", lastId)
xhr.send(null);
}

function longPollOnReadyStateChange(){
```

```
if(this.readyState != 4)return;
xhr = null;
longPollTimer = setTimeout(startLongPoll, 50);
processNonSSE(this.responseText);
}
```

When the onreadystatechange callback is called successfully, with data, xhr is set to null; this partners with the first line in startLongPoll(), which calls abort() if xhr has not been set to null. In normal operation, xhr will *always* be null when startLong Poll() is entered. It is only when it is called by a keep-alive timeout that xhr will not be null and instead will represent the previous connection. In other words, if the long-poll request does not reply within 20 seconds, abort it and make a fresh call.

Happy? I'm not. Long-poll has become not-very-long-poll. Every 20 seconds we make a new connection. They were expensive enough as it was. OK. So how about we never use keep-alive when using long-poll? To understand if that is good or not, think about the reasons we have keep-alive in the first place:

- To stop some intermediate server or router closing our socket.
- To keep retrying if the initial request failed.
- To detect when the backend has gone wrong in such a way that the socket is being kept open. (This also covers the case of intermittent browser bugs.)

The first point is moot if we are going to shut down the socket ourselves every 20 seconds. But the second and third points are good and noble reasons, and I wouldn't want to be without them in a production system. The third point is the troublesome one: there is simply no way to tell the difference between a server that has no message to send yet and a server that has gone into an infinite loop and is never going to reply. My suggestion is that you set a much higher number for keep-alive timeouts when using long-poll, because you don't ever really expect that crash, do you? You can do this by simply adding this line:

```
function startLongPoll(){
keepaliveSecs = 300;
if(xhr)xhr.abort();
...
```

For the second point (retrying if the initial request fails), see the next section.

Long-Poll and Connection Errors

Our previous long-poll code was rather optimistic: it assumed the URL was correct, and the server would always be happy to receive our request. What if the server is offline for any reason? Or if the URL is bad? When either of those happen, your longPollOnRea dyStateChange callback will quickly be called with readyState==4. You identify them by looking at the status element of the xhr object. Typical codes you will see are listed in Table 6-1.

Table 6-1. Common XMLHttpRequest status codes

Status code	Meaning
0	Connection issue, such as bad domain name
200	Success
304	It came from cache
401	Authentication failed
404	Server exists, but bad URL
500	Server error

I hope you never see a 304, because that would defeat the whole point of streaming live data! A 401 is intercepted by the browser, which asks the user for his credentials, then sends the request again. You only receive a 401 in your code if the user clicks Cancel. Therefore, we treat everything except a "200" status code as an error. For all errors, we assume no valid data was sent, and we sleep 30 seconds[2] before trying to long-poll again. Only when the status code is 200 do we use the data and immediately long-poll again. With these changes, the onreadystatechange callback now looks like this:

```
function longPollOnReadyStateChange(){
if(this.readyState != 4)return;
xhr = null;
if(this.status == 200){
  longPollTimer = setTimeout(startLongPoll, 50);
  processNonSSE(this.responseText);
  }
else{
  console.log("Connection failure, status:"+this.status);
  disconnect();
  longPollTimer = setTimeout(startLongPoll, 30000);
  }
}
```

The call to disconnect() stops a couple of timers (longpollTimer and the keep-alive timer) to make sure nothing else will call startLongPoll() before those 30 seconds are up.

---

2. This assumes keep-alive, when using long-poll, has been set to higher than 30 seconds. See "Long-Poll and Keep-Alive" on page 96. Otherwise the keep-alive will trigger first, which will then be interrupted by our 30-second timeout—which is not good.

If you really wanted to get clever, there are some status codes that have information in the payload. For instance, a 301 tells us a new URL we should try. A 305 tells us a proxy we should be using. If you are connecting to a third-party system, you may need to handle some of these; hopefully they will give you instructions on which ones. Watch out for 420 and 429, which tell you that you are making your connection attempts too frequently.

Server Side

Relative to the previous version of the server-side script (*fx_server.id.php*) we need a few changes. The first couple are specific to long-poll; at the very top of the script, see if "`longpoll`" has been requested by the client:

```
$GLOBALS["is_longpoll"] = array_key_exists("longpoll",$_POST)
  || array_key_exists("longpoll",$_GET);
$GLOBALS["is_sse"] = !($GLOBALS["is_longpoll"]);
```

This is a nice, compact expression to assign either `true` or `false` to $is_longpoll. It only tests for the existence of `longpoll` in the input data (either in GET or POST data), not for its value. The second line says if it is not long-poll, then it must be SSE. The other part of this change is at the very end of the main loop:

```
    ..
    if($GLOBALS["is_longpoll"])break;
    }
```

Short and sweet. Just like a honey bee drone: one package delivered, and then it kills itself.

I explicitly use the $GLOBALS[] array. This code and our main loop are both in the same scope (the global scope), so I could have assigned to the simpler $is_longpoll variable. But doing it this way means the code will still work if this code, or the main loop, gets refactored to its own function. It also documents the code: it screams "these are global variables" to the programmer who has to maintain this code in six months' time.

The other changes we make will be used for all our fallbacks. Previously you may remember we had these helper functions:

```
function sendData($data){
echo "data:";
echo json_encode($data)."\n";
echo "\n";
@flush();@ob_flush();
}
```

```
function sendIdAndData($data){
$id = $data["rows"][0]["id"];
echo "id:".json_encode($id)."\n";
sendData($data);
}
```

When we use the fallbacks, the bits specific to SSE (the data: prefix, the extra blank line at the end, and the separate id: row) are not needed, and in fact they get in the way. So why not drop them?

```
function sendData($data){
if($GLOBALS["is_sse"])echo "data:";
echo json_encode($data)."\n";
if($GLOBALS["is_sse"])echo "\n";
@flush();@ob_flush();
}

function sendIdAndData($data){
if($GLOBALS["is_sse"]){
  $id = $data["rows"][0]["id"];
  echo "id:".json_encode($id)."\n";
  }
sendData($data);
}
```

This means sendIdAndData() is now identical to sendData() for long-poll. That is fine. You can find this version as *fx_server.longpoll.php* in the book's source code. (If your server code sends retry:, you also need to do the same thing.)

 If you wanted to make a *polyfill*, you would not do this. Instead, on the client side you would strip off "data:" on lines that start with it, and you would look out for lines that start with anything else and ignore them.

One final change. Replace this line:

```
header("Content-Type: text/event-stream");
```

with:[3]

```
if($GLOBALS["is_sse"])header("Content-Type: text/event-stream");
else header("Content-Type: text/plain");
```

---

3. Did you think the Content-Type ought to be application/json instead of text/plain? The code we are writing here is for workarounds for browsers that are nowhere near the bleeding edge. Not the time for the semantic network soapbox. More seriously, the data we are sending is not strictly JSON. When we send 2+ data items together, it is two JSON strings separated by an LF. Each of those lines only turns into JSON inside the processOneLine() function.

Dealing with Data

Let's go back to the frontend and the `processNonSSE()` function we introduced earlier. This function is used in the next chapter, too. It does a couple of jobs that are done by the browser for us when using SSE:

```
function processNonSSE(msg){
var lines = msg.split(/\n/);
for(var ix in lines){
  var s = lines[ix];
  if(s.length == 0)continue;
  if(s[0] != "{"){
    s = s.substring(s.indexOf("{"));
    if(s.length == 0)continue;
  }
  processOneLine(s);
  }
}
```

To see the first job more clearly, here is a cut-down version:

```
function processNonSSE(msg){
var lines = msg.split(/\n/);
for(var ix in lines){
  processOneLine(lines[ix]);
  }
}
```

The SSE protocol always gives our callback exactly one message at a time. With long-poll we might have been given multiple messages.[4] So the preceding code breaks up the lines and processes each separately. But this cut-down version is naive and dangerous.

Our application protocol is exactly one JSON object per message, which also implies one line (CR and LF have to be escaped in JSON). But do you remember the SSE protocol? It finishes each message with a blank line. So the next thing we do is look for blank lines (`if(s.length == 0)`) and throw them away (`continue`).

What about the `if(s[0] != "{")` block? This is a Dirty Data Defense. `pro cess_one_line()` expects JSON, whole JSON, and nothing but JSON. If it gets anything else, it will throw an exception when it comes to parse it. In fact, it expects JSON representing an object, which means it must start with { and end with }. If there is any junk to the left of the opening curly bracket (`if(s[0] != "{")`), the `s.substring(s.index Of("{"))` line strips it away. And if that leaves nothing, then skip it completely. (By the way, this particular Dirty Data Defense was added as part of the iframe support of the next chapter; I've not seen long-poll trigger it.)

---

4. OK, *fx_server.longpoll.php* does not send multiple messages. But we could; look at the suggestions in "Optimizing Long-Poll" on page 92. And in the next chapter, multiple messages happen whether we want them to or not.

Wire It Up!

The last step is easy. Add the following highlighted line to `connect()`, then go and test it in a browser that does not support SSE:

```
function connect(){
gotActivity();
if(window.EventSource)start_eventsource();
else startLongPoll();
}
```

How do we test long-poll (or any of our later fallbacks) on a browser that already supports SSE? Rather than mess around with commenting clauses out, I recommend slapping some temporary code in at the top of the `connect()` function, like this:

```
function connect(){
gotActivity();

if(true)startLongPoll();else  //TEMP

if(window.EventSource)start_eventsource();
else startLongPoll();
}
```

I like to use those blank lines on each side, and the comment, to make it stand out and therefore hard to forget. (This temporary line to force long-poll is included in *fx_cli ent.longpoll.html*; please experiment with removing it.)

IE8 and Earlier

The code we have up to this point works fine in just about every browser, including Android 2.x. Sigh, not IE8. The only issue in IE8 is that `Object.keys` is not available. (This is used in the `makeHistoryTbody()` function introduced in "Adding a History Store" on page 51.) To add support, use the following block of code; insert it in the `<head>` of the page:

```
<script>
Object.keys=Object.keys || function(o,k,r){
  r=[];
  for(k in o)if(o.hasOwnProperty(k))r.push(k);
  return r;
  }
</script>
```

If `Object.keys` is natively supported, it will use that: `Object.keys=Object.keys`. Otherwise the rest of this block of code assigns a simple function to `Object.keys`, which iterates through the properties of the given object and adds them to an array. The `hasOwnProperty` is to avoid including any keys that have been added to the `Object` prototype. Search online or refer to an advanced JavaScript book if you want to understand that more deeply.

IE7 and Earlier

`Object.keys` was missing in IE6, IE7, and IE8. But there is still one more thing missing in IE6 and IE7: JSON. The `JSON` object is built into modern browsers (including IE8 and later) and gives us `parse()` and `stringify()` objects. Our code only needs `JSON.parse()`, so if you are seriously bandwidth-sensitive, you could strip down this solution. But this only affects IE6 and IE7 users, who by now must be so glad simply to find a website that still supports them that they won't care about an extra file load, so I am going to use the readily available *json2.js* file.

 This file is in the book's source code, or you can get it from *https:// github.com/douglascrockford/JSON-js*.

Actually I am using a minified version, which reduces the file from 17,530 to 3,377 bytes.

Now, IE6 and IE7 represent maybe 1% of your users, so it is unreasonable to expect the other 99% to have to download a patch that they don't need. (It does no harm; it is designed to only create the `JSON` object when one does not already exist, but it is a waste of bandwidth for both you and your users.) So I chose to use IE's special version detection. This is an IE-only feature (which actually disappeared as of IE10), but is ideal for our purposes:

```
<!--[if lte IE 7]>
<script src="json2.min.js"></script>
<![endif]-->
```

IE7 and earlier will process that `<script>` command and load, then run, *json2.min.js*. IE8 and IE9 will process the command but not do anything. All other browsers will just see this as an HTML comment and ignore it completely.

Overall, for all the modern browsers, including IE9 and later, we waste 198 bytes on patching IE8 and earlier. IE6 and IE7 have a further 3,377 bytes to load.

The Long and Winding Poll

In this chapter we have looked at more primitive mechanisms that can be used as an alternative to SSE. Regular polling might sometimes be a better choice than SSE if you only need sampling (as opposed to full history), or if latency is not important (e.g., if you can wait every 5 minutes for a batch of "latest" data; that way each client won't be holding open a socket). Then we looked at long-poll. Its great advantage is that it works on any OS/browser where Ajax works; and that is just about everywhere nowadays. Its disadvantage is that for every message received, there is an extra HTTP request involved. The good news is that for some browsers, there are more efficient choices—this is the subject of the next chapter.

CHAPTER 7

Fallbacks: There Has to Be a Better Way!

In the previous chapter we looked at long-poll as a way to push data from server to clients that do not support SSE. Its advantage over SSE is that it works just about everywhere, and its disadvantage is that the slightly higher latency and slightly higher bandwidth use can become significant for high-frequency updates. In this chapter we will look at two alternatives that are almost as good as native SSE, from the latency and bandwidth point of view.

The first fallback we look at uses Ajax, just as long-poll did, but using `readyState ==` `3`, instead of `readyState == 4`. In a nutshell it means we get each piece of data as the server pushes it out, while the connection is still alive, in contrast to long-poll where we don't see any of the data until the server closes the connection. (If you skipped over the sidebar "Ajax readyState" on page 91, this might be a fine time to go back and review what the Ajax `readyState` values mean.)

This is a nice approach, only slightly less efficient than SSE, so it is ironic that it gives us hardly any more desktop browser coverage.[1] Why? Because most of the browsers where it works already have native SSE support! However, this technique does work in Android 4.x (representing about two-thirds of Android users at the time of writing).

The second fallback is specifically for Internet Explorer 8 and above. There is nothing particularly IE-specific in the technique, so it is strange that it either does not work, or only works with some hacks in each of Firefox, Chrome, Safari, and Opera. But we already have native SSE for those browsers, so who cares? The key thing about this technique is that adding IE8/IE9/IE10 support gives us 28% more browser coverage.[2]

---

1. The only desktop browsers it adds for us are Firefox 3.x and Safari 3.x.

2. At the time of writing, and based on global stats. Also, you could say we already had IE8+ support, because the long-poll approach of Chapter 6 works, too. Rephrasing for pedants: for another 28% of users, it gives us a solution that is almost as efficient as native SSE.

Commonalities

As in Chapter 6, I will introduce the techniques as a minimal example first, before grafting them onto the FX demo. I will use the same backend for both techniques (XHR and iframe) that are being introduced in this chapter. See *abc_stream.php* in the book's source code, which looks like this:

```php
<?php
header("Content-Type: text/plain");

if(array_key_exists("HTTP_USER_AGENT",$_SERVER)
   && strpos($_SERVER["HTTP_USER_AGENT"],"Chrome/") !== false)
   echo str_repeat(" ",1023)."\n";
@ob_flush();@flush();

$ch = "A";
while(true){
  echo json_encode($ch.$ch)."\n";
  @ob_flush();@flush();
  if($ch == "Z")break;
  ++$ch;
  sleep(1);
  }
?>
```

We output the MIME type as `text/plain`. Note that we cannot use the `text/event-stream` that we use with SSE because browsers that don't support SSE don't know it, so they ask the user if they want to save it as a file!

The next line outputs exactly 1,024 bytes of whitespace. It is only needed for the Chrome browser, so here I use a user-agent check (`array_key_exists("HTTP_USER_AGENT",$_SERVER)` asks if we have been told a user-agent, and `strpos($string,$substring)! == false` is PHP's partial string-matching idiom, asking if $substring is found anywhere in $string).

After that, the rest of the code is easy: we output 26 strings, each one second apart. After 26 seconds we close the connection (simply so you can see how the browsers react when this happens). Just like in all the SSE code we created in earlier chapters, the `@ob_flush();@flush();` idiom is used to make sure the content is sent immediately and not buffered.

SSE has worked since Chrome 6, and it is one of the browsers that automatically upgrades itself, so realistically no one is still using a version of Chrome that needs any of these fallback techniques. But you will need this 1,024-bytes-of-whitespace code if you want to follow along with this chapter using Chrome. I also wanted to show this because it is a useful troubleshooting technique: when something does not work in a particular browser, a bunch of white-space can often work wonders.[3]

By the way, none of these buffering tricks could get any of the examples in this chapter to work with Opera 12! (But Opera has supported SSE since Opera 11.0, so we can live with that.)

On the frontend, one thing that both techniques introduced in this chapter have in common is that we don't get a new message each time the backend sends a new message. Instead, we get a long string holding *all messages since we connected*. This string gets longer and longer as time goes on. This creates two challenges for us:

- Extract just the new message(s).
- Avoid excessive memory usage.

For the first of those, we use the following function, where s is the full data received so far, prevOffset is where we have read up to so far (0 on the first call), and callback is the function that will process one message. The function returns the new furthest point processed, and that is what you pass in as prevOffset on the next call. If there was no new data, the input value of prevOffset ends up getting returned:

```
function getNewText(s,prevOffset,callback){
  if(!s)return prevOffset;
  var lastLF = s.lastIndexOf("\n") + 1;
  if(lastLF == 0 || prevOffset == lastLF)return prevOffset;
  var lines = s.substring(prevOffset,lastLF - 1).split(/\n/);
  for(var ix in lines)callback(lines[ix]);
  return lastLF; //Starting point for next time
  }
```

---

3. What is more, when prefixing, some whitespace does make a difference—it is a strong hint that there is browser optimization, typically caching, to blame.

On that theme, there is a way to get the XHR technique to work in Android 2.x, not just Android 4.x! Change the echo json_encode($ch.$ch)."\n"; line (which outputs exactly 3 bytes) to echo json_en code($ch.$ch).str_repeat(" ",1021)."\n";, (which outputs exactly 1,024 bytes). Yep, 2^{10} bytes. Smells like a buffer to me. But this is a really nasty hack, because every single message we send has to be padded. If the messages you want to send just happen to be that big, and you are latency sensitive, band-width sensitive, *and* sending quite frequent messages (meaning using long-poll for the Android 2.x users leaves you dissatisfied), then this may be just what you want. For the rest of us, it is better just to use long-poll for Android 2.x.

This also shows one other thing we have to be careful of (that SSE took care of for us, and was never an issue with long-polling): it is possible to get half a message. If you recall from Chapter 3, we decided on a protocol of one JSON message per line. If the server sends the message `{"x":3,"y":4}`\n, we will almost always receive `{"x":3,"y":4}`\n. But it is not *guaranteed*. We might get `{"x":3,"y`. Then a short while later our Ajax callback is called again and this time we get `":4}`\n, so that s now equals `{"x":3,"y":4}`\n. Once we know this might happen, of course, dealing with it is easy: simply look for the last LF in the input string, and ignore anything after that for the moment. That is what the `s.lastIndexOf("\n")` piece of JavaScript does. (The +1 is because it returns the index of the \n, and next time we want to start from just *after* that character.)

By comparing `prevOffset` with `lastLF`, we find out if we have any new data (which implies we have at least one whole new line). `s.substring(prevOffset,lastLF-1)` extracts just the new data. Then `.split(/\n/)` breaks it apart into one array entry per line. Finally, we can call our callback once for each line found.

What about the memory overflow challenge? This involves simply watching the size of the string, and once it gets rather large, killing the connection and reconnecting. You can decide the definition of "rather large" on a case-by-case basis, but I tend to use 32,768 unless I have a good reason not to. (What would be a good reason? For instance, if I was sending large blocks of data, and 32KB might fill up with just two or three messages.) This is not shown in our simple implementations for XHR and iframe, but will be shown when we graft them onto the FX application later in this chapter.

XHR

If you have already studied the long-poll code, there is not that much new to actually say about this code. We prepare an `XMLHttpRequest` object (because this code won't ever work with Internet Explorer 6, I don't bother with the check for `XMLHttpRequest` not being available), connecting to *abc_stream.php*, and setting the `onreadystatechange()` function. We call `send()` with a 50ms delay, for the sake of Safari (just as in the long-poll code); if we don't do this it all works, but it shows the "spinning circle" busy cursor all the time. We also add a custom variable to the xhr object, called `prevOffset`.

So, let's take a closer look at the `onreadystatechange` function. It does two things. First, it creates a log of each time it is called, which it appends to `<pre id="x">` (we use a `<pre>` so you can see the carriage returns). By the way, if we get called with no new content, it returns immediately. Then the last line of our `onreadystatechange` function uses `getNewText()`, which we developed earlier in this chapter. That will fill in `<p id="latest">` with the most recent line received. The code is as follows:

```
<!DOCTYPE html>
<html>
  <head>
    <meta charset="utf-8" />
    <title>Simple XHR Streaming Test</title>
    <script>
    function getNewText(s,prevOffset,callback){
      if(!s)return prevOffset;
      var lastLF = s.lastIndexOf("\n")+1;
      if(lastLF == 0 || prevOffset == lastLF)return prevOffset;
      var lines = s.substring(prevOffset, lastLF - 1).split(/\n/);
      for(var ix in lines)callback(lines[ix]);
      return lastLF; //Starting point for next time
      }

    function process(line){
      document.getElementById("latest").innerHTML = line;
      }
    </script>
  </head>
  <body>
    <p id="latest">Preparing...</p>
    <hr/>
    <pre id="x">Preparing...</pre>
    <script>
    var s="",s2prev="";
    var xhr = new XMLHttpRequest();
    xhr.prevOffset = 0;
    xhr.open("GET", "abc_stream.php");
    xhr.onreadystatechange = function(){
      var s2 = this.readyState + ":" +
        this.status + ":" + this.responseText;
      if(s2 == s2prev)return;
      s2prev = s2;
      s += s2 + "<br/>\n";
      document.getElementById("x").innerHTML = s;
      this.prevOffset = getNewText(
        this.responseText,this.prevOffset,process);
      };

    setTimeout(function(){xhr.send(null)}, 50);
    </script>

  </body>
</html>
```

So, put *simple_xhr_test.html* and *abc_stream.php* in the same directory, and open them in a supporting browser. You should see something like:

```
"CC"

1:0:
```

```
2:200:

3:200:"AA"

3:200:"AA"
"BB"

3:200:"AA"
"BB"
"CC"
```

After 26 seconds, you will see "ZZ" at the top of the screen. At the bottom, you will see these two sections:

```
3:200:"AA"
"BB"
"CC"
"DD"
...
"YY"
"ZZ"

4:200:"AA"
"BB"
"CC"
"DD"
...
"YY"
"ZZ"
```

You can see that you get all of "AA" to "ZZ" in readyState==3; then when the backend server shuts the connection, you get sent a readyState==4 signal, too.

This seems a good time to point out that opening *abc_stream.php* directly in most browsers has surprising behavior: you don't see "AA", then "AA" "BB". Instead it sits there doing nothing for 26 seconds, then suddenly shows all of "AA" to "ZZ". You only get to see the partially loaded data when using XMLHttpRequest. In fact, this is exactly why the iframe technique, which I'll introduce next, does not really work in those browsers.

iframe

The XHR technique shown in the previous section does not work in Internet Explorer: the problem is that IE does not set the xhr.responseText variable until xhr.ready State is 4! The whole point of the XHR technique was that the xhr.readyState never reaches 4. So this is a fatal blow. But all is not lost. The trick we use with Internet Explorer is to load that data into a dynamically created <iframe>, and then we go and look at the source of that iframe! The first time I heard that idea, I was so impressed I jumped out

---

of my chair and went to explain it to my cat. Yes, people deal with excitement in different ways. Cats too, as it turns out.

This fallback appears to work in most browsers, not just IE variants, but different browsers require a differing amount of data to be received from the server before they will make the data available. In IE6/7/8, only a few bytes need to be received before it starts working, and unless your messages are short, you should not need to worry about it.

But to follow along with this chapter in other browsers, you will need some extra hackery. In Chrome the requirement appears to be 1,024 bytes, just like it was in the XHR technique we looked at earlier. Our *abc_stream.php* script already sends out that much whitespace for Chrome. In Firefox it needs 2,048 bytes (so for a while I didn't realize this technique even worked in Firefox), which wasn't needed for the XHR technique. Add the highlighted line shown here to *abc_stream.php* to have it work immediately in Firefox too:

```
header("Content-Type: text/plain");

if(array_key_exists("HTTP_USER_AGENT", $_SERVER)
    && strpos($_SERVER["HTTP_USER_AGENT"], "Chrome/")!==false)
    echo str_repeat(" ",1023)."\n";
if(array_key_exists("HTTP_USER_AGENT", $_SERVER)
    && strpos($_SERVER["HTTP_USER_AGENT"], "Firefox/")!==false)
    echo str_repeat(" ",2047)."\n";
@ob_flush();@flush();

...
```

 Remember: I do not use the preceding code in the main FX application, because Chrome and Firefox will never need to use either the iframe or the XHR fallback techniques; they will always use native SSE. These hacks are just so you can follow along with this section without having to use Internet Explorer.

If you were paying attention, I casually mentioned that the data is available in IE6, IE7, and IE8. Hang on…didn't I say earlier that this technique only works in Internet Explorer 8? The problem is that Internet Explorer 7 and earlier do not allow us to access the contents of a child iframe from JavaScript. The test we can do to see if we can access an iframe's contents is:

```
if(window.postMessage){ /* OK */ }
```

`windows.postMessage` returns true in Internet Explorer 8 and above, false in Internet Explorer 7 and earlier.

The developer tools in IE10 and later have a compatibility mode that allows it to pretend it is IE9, IE8, or IE7. When it is pretending to be IE7, `windows.postMessage` returns true, meaning the iframe will appear to work in IE7. I believe this is a bug/limitation of IE10's compatibility mode, nothing more.

The iframe technique is inferior to the XHR technique in one particular way: we have to poll. But this is a different type of polling from that introduced in Chapter 6, because we are not polling the server. Instead, we are polling for changes in an iframe. It is completely localized polling, and relatively quick and light. But it still adds a bit of latency. In other words, the new messages get pushed from server to client immediately, but it takes us a little while to discover and process the new message. In the example shown here, we use `setInterval(...,500)`, which means we look for new messages every 500ms. So, the *mean* latency we add is 250ms. If we reduce the `setInterval` interval to 100ms, then the mean latency introduced is reduced to 50ms. The downside is more CPU use on the client for the extra polling. You need to balance the latency needs of your application against the desired CPU usage on the client. The code is as follows:

```
<!DOCTYPE html>
<html>
  <head>
    <meta charset="utf-8" />
    <title>Simple IFrame-Streaming Test</title>
    <script>
    function getNewText(s,prevOffset,callback){
      if(!s)return prevOffset;
      var lastLF = s.lastIndexOf("\n")+1;
      if(lastLF == 0 || prevOffset == lastLF)return prevOffset;
      var lines = s.substring(prevOffset, lastLF - 1).split(/\n/);
      for(var ix in lines)callback(lines[ix]);
      return lastLF; //Starting point for next time
      }
    </script>
  </head>
  <body>
    <p id="latest">Preparing...</p>
    <hr/>
    <pre id="x">Preparing...</pre>
    <script>
    function connectIframe(){
    iframe = document.createElement("iframe");
    iframe.setAttribute("style", "display: none;");
    iframe.setAttribute("src", "abc_stream.php");
    document.body.appendChild(iframe);
    var prevOffset = 0;
    setInterval(function(){
      var s = iframe.contentWindow.document.body.innerHTML;
```

```
        prevOffset = getNewText(s,prevOffset,function(line){
          document.getElementById("latest").innerHTML = line;
          });
        document.getElementById("x").innerHTML = s;
        }, 500);
      }

      if(window.postMessage){
        document.getElementById("x").innerHTML = "OK";
        setTimeout(connectIframe, 100);
        }
      else{
        document.getElementById("x").innerHTML = "Sorry!";
        }
      </script>

    </body>
  </html>
```

Starting at the bottom of this code, we look for `window.postMessage`, and if it exists we call `connectIframe()`: there has to be a 100ms delay, otherwise we get an HTML parsing error when we try to create the iframe. In `connectIframe`, the first four lines create an `<iframe>` dynamically, with `display:none` CSS to make it invisible, and the `src` set to our streaming data source. Then we use `setInterval` to set up a regular timer, and every 500ms we fetch the contents of the iframe. Just as in the XHR demo in the previous section, we put all contents so far in the `"x"` element, and just the most recent message in the `"latest"` element.

Put *simple_iframe_test.html* in the same directory as *abc_stream.php* and open it in IE8 or above, and you should see the "latest" element changing every second.

Grafting XHR/Iframe onto Our FX Application

The steps to do this will be very similar to how we grafted long-poll onto the FX application in Chapter 6. There are some minor backend changes, and we add some frontend code that looks like the simple code introduced earlier in this chapter, as well as the feature-detection code to wire it up.

XHR on the Backend

Do you remember this code from Chapter 6?

```
$GLOBALS["is_longpoll"] = array_key_exists("longpoll",$_POST)
  || array_key_exists("longpoll",$_GET);
$GLOBALS["is_sse"] = !($GLOBALS["is_longpoll"]);
```

Our clients (both XHR and iframe) will identify themselves as using XHR, so modify it as follows:

```
$GLOBALS["is_longpoll"] = array_key_exists("longpoll",$_POST)
   || array_key_exists("longpoll",$_GET);
$GLOBALS["is_xhr"] = array_key_exists("xhr",$_POST)
   || array_key_exists("xhr",$_GET);
$GLOBALS["is_sse"] = !($GLOBALS["is_longpoll"] || $GLOBALS["is_xhr"]);
```

There is nothing else to do server side. The format of the data that is pushed is identical to that using long-poll. Basically xhr is given solely to set the correct MIME type (text/plain and not text/event-stream, because the latter will cause some browsers to prompt for the user to save it to an external file). (The file with the preceding addition is found in the book's source code as *fx_server.xhr.php*).

XHR on the Frontend

Add the following block of code to the *fx_client.longpoll.html* file we had as of the end of the previous chapter:

```
function getNewText(s,prevOffset){
if(!s)return prevOffset;
var lastLF = s.lastIndexOf("\n") + 1;
if(lastLF == 0 || prevOffset == lastLF)return prevOffset;
var lines = s.substring(prevOffset, lastLF - 1).split(/\n/);
for(var ix in lines)processNonSSE(lines[ix]);
return lastLF; //Starting point for next time
}

function startXHR(){
if(xhr)xhr.abort();
xhr = new XMLHttpRequest();
xhr.prevOffset = 0;
xhr.onreadystatechange = function(){
  this.prevOffset = getNewText(
    this.responseText,this.prevOffset);
  };
var u = url;
u += "xhr=1&t=" + (new Date().getTime());
xhr.open("GET", u);
if(last_id)xhr.setRequestHeader("Last-Event-ID", last_id)
xhr.send(null);
}
```

The getNewText function is as we saw earlier, but instead of taking a callback as a parameter we hardcode processNonSSE() as the callback. This is used for both the XHR and iframe techniques (and, you may remember, is also being used by long-poll). The startXHR() function is similar to the simple example we made earlier in the chapter, but ironically it is actually simpler: there is no messing around reporting the various xhr.readyState values; we use one line to process them all. When readyState is 0, 1, or 2, responseText is empty, so getNewText will do nothing (and return 0). Note that it copes with the case where `xhr.responseText` is `null`. `xhr` is a private variable, of the SSE object, that was defined in the previous chapter.

If the server closes the connection and `readyState` is 4, then there are two possible situations. Either there was no new data since the last call to `onreadystatechange`, or there was new data (perhaps we had previously received half a message, and were just waiting for the final few bytes and the LF). Either way, `getNewText()` does the right thing. It is the kind of function you can take home to meet the family, without having to worry about it embarrassing you.

Iframe on the Frontend

First add another private variable to our SSE object, next to where we define `es` and `xhr`:

```
var iframe = null;
```

 As mentioned in the previous chapter, es, xhr, and `iframe` are exclusive, meaning they could all be named `server`, or something, and share the same variable. I chose to use three distinct private variables in this book for code clarity.

Then add this function:

```
function startIframe(){
var u = url;
u += "xhr=1&t=" + (new Date().getTime());
iframe = document.createElement("iframe");
iframe.setAttribute("style", "display: none;");
iframe.setAttribute("src", u);
document.body.appendChild(iframe);
var prevOffset = 0;
setInterval(function(){
  if(!iframe.contentWindow.document.body)return;
  var s = iframe.contentWindow.document.body.innerHTML;
  prevOffset=getNewText(s, prevOffset);
  }, 500);
}
```

This is basically the same code we saw earlier in the chapter, but using the global URL, and with the logging code cut out. It needs a bit of enhancing to be production-ready, though. First pass the `lastId` variable (done in the URL, not as a header). The other changes, shown next, are to tidy up from a previous call when this function is called a second time (and you remember that happens when our keep-alive mechanism has had to kick in):

```
function startIframe(){
if(iframe)iframe.parentNode.removeChild(iframe);
if(iframeTimer)clearInterval(iframeTimer);
var u = url;
if(last_id)u += "last_id="
  + encodeURIComponent(last_id) + "&";
u += "xhr=1&t=" + (new Date().getTime());
iframe = document.createElement("iframe");
iframe.setAttribute("style", "display: none;");
iframe.setAttribute("src", u);
document.body.appendChild(iframe);
var prevOffset = 0;
iframeTimer = setInterval(function(){
    var s = iframe.contentWindow.document.body.innerHTML;
    prevOffset = getNewText(s, prevOffset);
    }, 500);
}
```

This also needs one more private variable: `var iframeTimer = null;`.

Wiring Up XHR

The `connect()` function currently looks like:

```
function connect(){
gotActivity();
if(window.EventSource)startEventSource();
else startLongPoll();
}
```

Add this line:

```
function connect(){
gotActivity();
if(window.EventSource)startEventSource();
else if(window.XMLHttpRequest &&
  typeof new XMLHttpRequest().responseType != "undefined")
  startXHR();
else startLongPoll();
}
```

The browser detection is a little complicated. What we need for this to work is XMLHttpRequest2 (*http://www.w3.org/TR/XMLHttpRequest2/*). The first part of the change to the function checks if `XMLHttpRequest` is defined. Just about every single browser will return true for this, as this is defined in the first version of XHR. When XHR got a bunch of new features the designers decided against calling the enhanced object `XMLHttpRequest2`, so it is still called `XMLHttpRequest`. Unfortunately they also decided against any kind of version number. There is also no object directly related to the XMLHttpRequest2 functionality we are using. Humbug. So, we are left with testing by coincidence: all browsers[4] that define a `responseType` element on their `XMLHttpRe quest` objects also give us access to the `responseText` data in `readyState==3`.

 To force using XHR on browsers that support SSE, for testing purposes, put this at the top of `connect()`:

```
if(true)startXHR();else
```

Wiring Up Iframe

If you thought the feature detection for XHR was complicated, you ain't seen nothing yet. The feature detection for the iframe technique is in two parts. The first part goes at the top of the HTML file. We met Internet Explorer's special macro language in the previous chapter. Here we use it to set a JavaScript global to true for IE9 and earlier, and false for everyone else. (We don't use iframe for IE10 and later because the XHR technique works, which is lucky because the special IE macro language no longer does!) Near the top of the <head> part of the HTML file add the highlighted code (the other code shown here is what we already had in *fx_client.longpoll.html*):

```
<script>var isIE9OrEarlier = false;</script>
<!--[if lte IE 7]>
<script src="json2.min.js"></script>
<![endif]-->
<!--[if lte IE 9]>
<script>
isIE9OrEarlier = true;
</script>
<![endif]-->
<script>
Object.keys=Object.keys || function(o,k,r){
  r = [];
  for(k in o)if(o.hasOwnProperty(k))r.push(k);
  return r;
  }
</script>
```

Now with our new `isIE9OrEarlier` global in our grubby little hands, add the following lines to `connect()`:

```
function connect(){
gotActivity();
if(window.EventSource)start_eventsource();
else if(isIE9OrEarlier){
    if(window.postMessage)startIframe();
```

---

4. Okay, all browsers that I have tried it on. Remember, out there in the real world this fallback is only going to be used by Android 4.x, and this feature detection works without problems there.

```
    else startLongPoll();
    }
else if(window.XMLHttpRequest &&
  typeof new XMLHttpRequest().responseType != "undefined")
  startXHR();
else startLongPoll();
}
```

In plain English: if IE9 and earlier, then either use iframe (i.e., IE8 and IE9, because only they have the `window.postMessage` function defined) or long-poll (i.e., for IE5.5, IE6, and IE7). If IE10 or IE11, then fall through and use XHR instead.

 For completeness I should tell you that to force testing of the iframe technique on browsers that support SSE, put this at the top of con nect():

```
if(true)startIframe();else
```

One more change is to add a couple more clauses to the `disconnect()` function:

```
function disconnect(){
if(keepaliveTimer){
  clearTimeout(keepaliveTimer);
  keepaliveTimer = null;
  }
if(es){
  es.close();
  es = null;
  }
if(xhr){
  xhr.abort();
  xhr = null;
  }
if(longPollTimer){
  clearTimeout(longPollTimer);
  longPollTimer = null;
  }
if(iframeTimer){
  clearTimeout(iframeTimer);
  iframeTimer = null;
  }
if(iframe){
  iframe.parentNode.removeChild(iframe);
  iframe = null;
  }
}
```

Thanks for the Memories

What was it I forgot? I'm sure there was something. Sigh, my memory just gets worse... that was it! Memory management! Both the XHR and iframe approaches are storing all messages sent by the server; basically it is one big message under the surface. This wasn't a problem with SSE because the EventSource object treats each message separately, and wasn't a problem with long-poll because each message was a complete connection. If you run a script for long enough, it is going to be a problem for XHR and iframe, though: the buffer is going to keep getting larger and larger until it starts to drag down the client system.

The solution is as simple as it is crude: when the one big message gets too big, make a fresh connection. There are some downsides, and it is fair to say that the lack of this issue is the biggest advantage native SSE has over the XHR fallback. Before examining the downsides, let's look at the code. It involves the addition of code to getNewText() (which is used by both XHR and iframe, but not used by native SSE and not used by long-poll), and nowhere else:

```
function getNewText(s,prevOffset){
var lastLF = s.lastIndexOf("\n")+1;
if(lastLF == 0 || prevOffset == lastLF)return prevOffset;
var lines = s.substring(prevOffset, lastLF - 1).split(/\n/);
for(var ix in lines)processNonSSE(lines[ix]);

if(lastLF > 65536){
  console.log("Received " + lastLF +
    " bytes (" + s.length + "). Will reconnect.");
  disconnect();
  setTimeout(connect, 1);
  }

return lastLF; //Starting point for next time
}
```

In other words, once the buffer is over 64KB, disconnect, then connect again. The call to connect() is done on a 1ms timer just to avoid potential problems with recursive calls.

The first downside to point out is that the choice of 64KB is arbitrary. It takes about 2.5 minutes for the FX demo to fill it. If each message is bigger, or the messages come through more quickly, you might want to increase the buffer size. If all your users are on desktop machines, you could increase it by 10 times or more; even on a mobile device, 64KB is not *that* big.

The second downside is that any half-messages get lost—remember the discussion from earlier that led us to use `s.lastIndexOf("\n")`. These half-messages are going to be rare (hopefully), so you could change the condition to be `if(lastLF > 65536 && lastLF == s.length)`, telling it to always wait for a clean point to break the connection. Just bear in mind that this means that theoretically it could never disconnect (causing a memory issue).

The third issue is the same problem we had with long-poll: we might miss a message during the time between the disconnect and the next connect. However, if we send the `lastId` received (as we do in the FX demo), then the second and third downsides become neutralized: we don't end up missing anything, and all we have is a bit of inefficiency.

Putting the FX Baby to Bed

And so that finishes the FX application we have been developing over the past five chapters—99+% browser coverage, with the most efficient available technique we can find for each of those users (if you lost track of which users are using which technique, see Table 7-1 in the following sidebar), for a realistically complex data-push application, dealing with production issues like servers and sockets disappearing on us, scheduled shutdowns, and more.

In Chapter 9, the FX application will be revived when we look at authentication and other security-related issues. But before that, there are a few aspects of SSE that we have not used, and these will be covered in the next chapter.

Who Ends Up Where?

Table 7-1 summarizes how the browser detection works.

Table 7-1. Which start() function to use, based on user's browser

Function	Browser
startEventSource()	<ul><li>Basically all Firefox and Chrome[a]</li><li>Desktop Safari 5.0+</li><li>iOS Safari 4.0+</li><li>Android 4.4+ (earlier where Chrome is default browser)</li><li>Chrome for Android (all versions)</li><li>Firefox for Android (all versions)</li><li>Opera since 11.0</li><li>Opera Mobile since 11.1</li><li>BlackBerry since 7.0</li></ul>
startXHR()	<ul><li>IE10+</li><li>Firefox 3.6 (and earlier)</li><li>Safari 3.x</li><li>Android 4.1 to 4.3 (unless Chrome is default browser)</li><li>Android 3.x</li></ul>
startIframe()	<ul><li>IE8</li><li>IE9</li></ul>
startLongpoll()	<ul><li>IE6</li><li>IE7</li><li>Android 2.x</li><li>Anything else not in the preceding list that has Ajax support</li></ul>
(none)	<ul><li>Any browser with JavaScript disabled</li></ul>

[a] Technically since Firefox 6 and Chrome 6, but they have been auto-updating since Firefox 4, and Chrome since it came out of beta, so you can reasonably expect no one is still using versions that do not support SSE.

CHAPTER 8

More SSE: The Rest of the Standard

The SSE standard contains a few other features that I have glossed over in this book, and this chapter will take a look at them. These other features of SSE have been ignored for a couple of reasons. First, I didn't need them! By making the decision to always pass around one JSON object per line, and having the JSON object be self-descriptive, the *event* and *multiline* features were never needed. The second reason is that it would have made the fallbacks slower and more complicated. By being pragmatic and not trying to create a perfect polyfill of SSE, we could allow our fallbacks to use the protocol that best suited them. But it is good to know about them, and this chapter will introduce each feature, show when you might want to use it, and even give some hints as to how to implement it in our fallbacks.

Headers

Here is a simple script (found as *log_headers.html* in the book's source code):

```
<html>
  <head>
    <title>Logging test</title>
  </head>
  <body>
    <script>
    var es = new EventSource("log_headers.php");
    </script>
  </body>
</html>
```

This goes to show just how small an SSE script can be. Of course, it does absolutely nothing on the frontend. Here is the corresponding backend script:

```
<?php
$SSE = (@$_SERVER["HTTP_ACCEPT"] == "text/event-stream");
if($SSE)
```

```
    header("Content-Type: text/event-stream");
else
    header("Content-Type: text/plain");
file_put_contents("tmp.log", print_r($_SERVER, true) );
?>
```

This is also embarrassingly short. It simply writes everything it finds in the superglobal $_SERVER to a file called *tmp.log*. This includes the HTTP headers that the browser sent to the server, which is usually what we are interested in. *tmp.log* only shows the most recent request; it is overwritten each time. Try it out with each of your target browsers.

 If *tmp.log* does not get created when accessed through a web server, it is probably write permissions. On a Unix system, run touch tmp.log then chmod 666 tmp.log. Then try again.

I wanted to show this one first, because you can take that file_put_con tents("tmp.log",print_r($_SERVER,true)); line and put it at the top of any script that you want to troubleshoot, or just understand.

If you want to also see the contents of COOKIES, POST and all the other superglobals, it is trivial to add them, too. However, even better is to show the output of phpinfo(), an excerpt of which is shown in Figure 8-1. I will not show the script here because it is quite PHP-specific, but take a look at *show_phpinfo.php* if you are curious.

The *show_phpinfo.php* script grabs phpinfo() output (which is in HTML), does a little formatting, then outputs it as an SSE block. It wraps it in a JSON string to make sure the line breaks don't cause problems. (The code also works with the XHR and long-poll fallbacks, and also includes some of the headers we look at in this chapter, to make it more generally useful.) Here is what the frontend looks like:

```
<html>
  <head>
    <title>PHPInfo Test</title>
  </head>
  <body>
    <div id="x">(loading...)</div>
    <script>
    var es = new EventSource("show_phpinfo.php");
    es.addEventListener("message", function(e){
      var s = JSON.parse(e.data);
      document.getElementById("x").innerHTML = s;
      },false);
    </script>
  </body>
</html>
```

apc.slam_defense	On	On
apc.stat	On	On
apc.stat_ctime	Off	Off
apc.ttl	0	0
apc.use_request_time	On	On
apc.user_entries_hint	4096	4096
apc.user_ttl	0	0
apc.write_lock	On	On

APD

Advanced PHP Debugger (APD)	Enabled
APD Version	1.0.1

bcmath

BCMath support	enabled

Directive	Local Value	Master Value
bcmath.scale	0	0

bz2

BZip2 Support	Enabled
Stream Wrapper support	compress.bz2://
Stream Filter support	bzip2.decompress, bzip2.compress
BZip2 Version	1.0.5, 10-Dec-2007

calendar

Calendar support	enabled

Core

PHP Version	5.3.2-1ubuntu4.21

Directive	Local Value	Master Value
allow_call_time_pass_reference	Off	Off
allow_url_fopen	On	On
allow_url_include	Off	Off
always_populate_raw_post_data	Off	Off
arg_separator.input	&	&
arg_separator.output	&	&
asp_tags	Off	Off
auto_append_file	no value	no value
auto_globals_jit	On	On
auto_prepend_file	no value	no value
browscap	no value	no value

Figure 8-1. Sample output of show_phpinfo.html

If you see "(loading...)" and nothing else, you are likely getting a 403 Forbidden for the access to *show_phpinfo.php*. See the following warning block for why.

Do not put this particular script on a production server. phpin fo() goes into great detail about your system, and some of it could be useful to a hacker.

Because people might upload all the book's source code to their web server before they read this chapter, an *.htaccess* file is included that specifically blocks access to *show_phpinfo.php*, using this block:

```
<Files "show_phpinfo.php">
    deny from all
</Files>
```

On a system *where you are confident that the outside world will not have access*, you can go ahead and delete that block from the *.htac cess* file.

Note that *.htaccess* files will only work if your Apache configuration is set to allow their use. Sometimes they are disabled for reasons of either performance or central control. Changing AllowOverride to All or at least AllowOverride AuthConfig Limit in your Apache configuration files will do the job. See *https://httpd.apache.org/docs/2.0/mod/core.html#allowoverride* for more information.

See "Authorization (with Apache)" on page 137 in Chapter 9 for more on using the *.htaccess* file to control access to SSE resources.

Most other languages supply the same access to the headers. Here is how to do it with a standalone Node.js server:

```
var http = require("http");

http.createServer(function(request,response){
  console.log(request.method+" "+request.url);
  console.log(request.headers);

  if(request.url!="/sse"){
    response.end("<html>"+
      "<head><title>Logging test</title></head>"+
      "<body><script>"+
      "var es = new EventSource('/sse');"+
      "</script></body></html>\n");
    return;
    }

  response.writeHead(200,
    { "Content-Type": "text/plain" });
  response.end();
  }).listen(1234);
```

Start this with node log_headers.node.js, and it will listen on port 1234 on all IP addresses of your server. The key line is console.log(request.headers);. It outputs to the console, but you could easily change this to log to a file, as the PHP example did.

The rest of the script is scaffolding to send back an HTML file that can call the server again using SSE. Also of interest might be the `console.log(request.method+" "+re quest.url);` line, to show which file was requested.

Event

As we have seen throughout the book, the server prefixes the data to send with `data:`. Then on the client side this is received by creating a handler for the `message` event:

```
es.addEventListener("message", function(e){
    var d = JSON.parse(e.data);
    document.getElementById(d.symbol).innerHTML = d.bid;
    },false);
```

It turns out that the `message` is the default, and you can have the server label each line of data in such a way that a different function can be used to take care of it on the frontend.

The labeling is done with an `event:` line preceding the data. Then on the client side it is handled by specifying a handler for just that kind of event. An example will make this clear. Going back to the FX application, the data could have been sent like this:

```
event:AUD/GBP
data:{"timestamp":"2014-02-28 06:49:55.081","bid":"1.47219","ask":"1.47239"}

event:USD/JPY
data:{"timestamp":"2014-02-28 06:49:56.222","bid":"94.956","ask":"94.966"}

event:EUR/USD
data:{"timestamp":"2014-02-28 06:49:56.790","bid":"1.30931","ask":"1.30941"}

event:EUR/USD
data:{"timestamp":"2014-02-28 06:49:57.002","bid":"1.30983","ask":"1.30993"}

event:EUR/USD
data:{"timestamp":"2014-02-28 06:49:57.450","bid":"1.30972","ask":"1.30982"}

event:AUD/GBP
data:{"timestamp":"2014-02-28 06:49:57.987","bid":"1.47235","ask":"1.47255"}

event:AUD/GBP
data:{"timestamp":"2014-02-28 06:49:58.345","bid":"1.47129","ask":"1.47149"}
```

Compare this with the first code block in "Fine-Grained Timestamps" on page 39. If you are very bandwidth-sensitive, using `event:` like this appears to save 6 bytes per message. However, by changing "symbol" to "s" in our original JSON, it would be a mere 1-byte difference, and if we were using CSV instead of JSON, then using `event:` would be 7 bytes more expensive.

The event name can be made up of any Unicode characters, except carriage return and line feed. If you need multiline event names, first find a mirror and ask yourself: "*Really?*" If the answer is still yes, then work out some escaping mechanism—for instance, JSON-encoding event names and then using the encoded version in your call to `addE ventListener`.

On the client side, instead of the "message" handler shown earlier, I instead create a handler for each possible "event." In this case that means one event handler for each FX symbol:

```
es.addEventListener("EUR/USD", function(e){
  var d = JSON.parse(e.data);
  document.getElementById("EUR/USD").innerHTML = d.bid;
  },false);

es.addEventListener("USD/JPY", function(e){
  var d = JSON.parse(e.data);
  document.getElementById("USD/JPY").innerHTML = d.bid;
  },false);

es.addEventListener("AUD/GBP", function(e){
  var d = JSON.parse(e.data);
  document.getElementById("AUD/GBP").innerHTML = d.bid;
  },false);
```

I am sure that made you cringe, throw up your hands, and scream, "Yuck!" Yes. When the data being multiplexed (FX symbols in this case) is the *same format*, and processed in the *same way*, using `event:` for each data stream is going to cost you more than it gains. It was a bad example...I'm sorry.

A better example? Well, one where the data for each "event" is going to be processed in a different way. How about a chat application? It is reasonable to imagine this kind of data stream being sent:

```
event:enter
data:{id:17653,name:"Sweet Suzy"}

event:message
data:{msg:"Hello everyone!",from:17563}

event:exit
data:1465
```

The chat messages are sent as JSON. The JSON has a `msg` field for the actual chat message and a `from` field with the ID of the user who sent it. When members enter the chat room they are announced with an `enter` event, which gives the user ID, and information about them (here just their name). When members leave the chat room, an `exit` message is sent and the data is just their numeric ID, not a JSON object:

```
es.addEventListener("enter",
  function(e){ addMember(JSON.parse(e.data)); },false);
es.addEventListener("exit",
  function(e){ removeMember(e.data); },false);
es.addEventListener("message",
  function(e){ addMessage(JSON.parse(e.data)); },false);
```

We use the following functions to do the actual work:

```
function addMember(d){
  members[d.id] = d;
  var img = document.createElement("img");
  img.id = "member_img_" + d.id;
  img.alt = d.name;
  img.src = "/img/members/" + d.id + ".png";
  document.getElementById("memberimg").appendChild(img);
  }

function removeMember(id){
  var img = document.getElementById("member_img_" + id);
  img.parentNode.removeChild(img);
  delete members[id];
  }

function addMessage(d){
  var msg = document.createElement("div");
  msg.innerHTML = d.msg;
  document.getElementById("messages").appendChild(msg);
  }
```

 addMessage() could use d.from. I've also skipped over error checking; be careful with this code in production because it allows a Java-
Script injection attack (though the server should be taking care of
stripping out bad tags from the chat messages).

How can the fallbacks be made to work with event: lines? One way is to add some code
to our earlier processNonSSE(msg) (see "Dealing with Data" on page 101). We will also
need a global to remember which event is being processed currently:

```
var currentEvent = null;
...
function processNonSSE(msg){
var lines = msg.split(/\n/);
for(var ix in lines){
  var s = lines[ix];
  if(s.length == 0)continue;
  if(s.indexOf("event:") == 0){
    currentEvent = s.substring(6);
    }
  else{
```

```
        if(currentEvent == "exit"){
          removeMember(s);
          }
        else{
          if(s[0] != "{"){
            s = s.substring(s.indexOf("{"));
            if(s.length == 0)continue;
            }
          var d = JSON.parse(s);
          if(currentEvent == "enter")
            addMember(d);
          else if(currentEvent == "message")
            addMessage(d);
          //else unknown event
          }
        }
      }
    }
```

Notice that some of the complexity here is because of not using a JSON object for all events. This is one reason I suggest just settling on using a JSON object for all data; it makes dealing with the fallbacks easier.

That is one way. The other way is to add an event field to the JSON object (again, this requires changing the "exit" event to use a JSON object). This resembles the way we used the id: row for SSE clients, but also repeated the "id" information in the JSON object (see "Sending Last-Event-ID" on page 71).

But if we are going to do that, why bother with using the event row at all? We end up with all messages coming through processOneLine(s) and the code looks a bit like this:

```
switch(d){
  case "enter":addMember(d);break;
  case "exit":removeMember(d.id);break;
  case "message":addMessage(d);break;
  }
```

So, to sum up, the event: feature of SSE is one way to organize different actions, but it offers no advantages over doing it yourself with an extra JSON or CSV field, and doing it that way makes dealing with other browsers easier and more efficient. So I suggest you only use event: when both these conditions are true:

- All your clients have native SSE support.
- You want to use a mix of different data types for your event types, including some simple data types such as integer, float, or string (and therefore including your own event field is not possible).

Multiline Data

Throughout the book I have advocated using JSON objects for message passing. One of the reasons for that it is gave us one exactly line per message. Why is that a benefit? Because it makes it very easy to do the parsing in the fallbacks used by the older browsers.

Did you notice how in the FX application the backend only sent an extra carriage return after the data when in SSE mode? When using long-poll, XHR, or iframe techniques, it skipped this because we didn't need it: one line of JSON is always a complete message. (Incidentally, we saved one byte, or actually six bytes, because the fallbacks did not prefix the data lines with `data:` either. Saving 6 bytes was *not* the reason this was done. Saving some client-side processing was.)

So why does SSE require that extra blank line between messages? It is there because the SSE standard allows for a message to be split across multiple lines. For example, the server can send this data:

```
data:Roses are red
data:Violets are blue
data:No need to escape
data:When you do as I do
                        <-- Extra LF
```

For the sake of understanding how the client will deal with it, let's pretend that the server flushes the data after each line, then goes to sleep for a second or two. The client will receive "Roses are red." No blank line has been received, so it buffers it up and waits. Two seconds later it gets a second line, "Violets are blue," so it buffers this: "Roses are red\nViolets are blue." Notice that it is just buffering—it is not telling the client that any data has arrived yet. After the fourth line it has buffered up "Roses are red\nViolets are blue\nNo need to escape\nWhen you do as I do." Finally, the client gets a blank line. It calls the JavaScript event handler passing the single long string built up in its buffer.

The string passed to the event handler does not have the final LF.

(The standard says clients should go to the trouble of adding an LF after each line when it buffers it up, only to then remove the final one at the end. Standards do things like that, and often find themselves alone at parties, with no one to talk to but the potted plant in the corner.)

What if you really wanted a blank line at the end of your message? Send a blank `data:` line. For instance, the following sequence will pass the string "111\n\n333\n\n" to the event handler:

```
data:111
data:
data:333
data:
data:
```

Why does SSE let us do this? It does it so that there is no need to escape carriage returns. In contrast when we use JSON, the above poem looks like this:

```
data:"Roses are red\nViolets are blue\nNo need to escape\nWhen you do as I do"
```

Unlike in the buffer example earlier in this section, \n refers to two bytes, first a \, then an n. Including the `data:` and the following blank line, the JSON string is 80 bytes, whereas the non-JSON version is 91 bytes. All those `data:` strings added up to more than the extra byte for the \, and the extra two bytes for the quotes.

 How do we implement handling multiple lines for a single message in the fallbacks? Basically you would have to implement the SSE buffering algorithm described earlier in this section, in JavaScript. And the server has to send that extra blank line for all clients, not just the SSE clients. This is not that hard, and you wouldn't need to use the `data:` prefix, so the byte difference would not be against you. But when this approach is compared to the ease of always using one line of JSON, I feel you would need a jolly good reason to want to go down this path.

In summary, use the multiline feature of SSE when all these conditions are true:

- All your clients have native SSE support.
- You have naturally multiline data to send.
- You have a good reason not to use JSON.

Whitespace in Messages

This is a quick, short section. Throughout the book I have used `data:XXX`, `event:XXX`, etc. The standard also allows you to write `data: XXX`, `event: XXX`, etc. In other words, you can have a space after the colon. I am an easygoing person, happy to let people choose their own way of doing things, but I'm going to take a stand here: *never do this.* It just wastes a byte, and has no advantage whatsoever.

But this feature creates a potential problem: if you are sending raw strings as your data, if you ever need to have a leading space in your data, it will get sucked away. What to do? The simple solution is to use JSON. Gosh, I do keep harping on about that, don't I! The downside is minor: two extra bytes per string (for the quotes), as well as an extra escape slash character if your string has any special characters. But that is still a downside; is there another solution? Yes. If you want to send raw strings, and there is the chance of an important leading space, then prefix all strings with a space. It wastes one byte per line. If that waste still bothers you, only do this when your data has a leading space…but that is a lot of fuss for the sake of a byte.

Headers Again

In the FX application, I passed in xhr=1 or longpoll=1 in the URL so that the server could identify the fallback. We then identified SSE as the absence of either of those. There is another way. But before we look at it, here is a reminder of how those are used:

longpoll

>   Send a text/plain content-type header; exit after sending a message.

xhr

>   Send a text/plain content-type header.

sse

>   Send a text/event-stream content-type header.
>
>   Send a data: prefix, an extra carriage return, and id: lines.

The alternative way is that SSE clients will send an Accept: text/event-stream header, which should uniquely identify them as supporting SSE natively. So the FX application had these lines:

```
$GLOBALS["is_longpoll"] = array_key_exists("longpoll", $_POST)
  || array_key_exists("longpoll", $_GET);
$GLOBALS["is_xhr"] = array_key_exists("xhr", $_POST)
  || array_key_exists("xhr", $_GET);
$GLOBALS["is_sse"]=!($GLOBALS["is_longpoll"] || $GLOBALS["is_xhr"]);

...

if($GLOBALS["is_sse"])header("Content-Type: text/event-stream");
else header("Content-Type: text/plain");
```

By instead using that header, there is no longer a need to send xhr=1; there is still a need to send longpoll=1 though, so the difference between that and XHR/iframe can be detected. The code ends up looking something like this:

```
$GLOBALS["is_sse"] = @$_SERVER["HTTP_ACCEPT"] == "text/event-stream";
$GLOBALS["is_longpoll"] = array_key_exists("longpoll", $_POST)
  || array_key_exists("longpoll", $_GET);
$GLOBALS["is_xhr"]=!($GLOBALS["is_longpoll"] || $GLOBALS["is_sse"]);

...

if($GLOBALS["is_sse"])header("Content-Type: text/event-stream");
else header("Content-Type: text/plain");
```

You have perhaps spotted why I didn't do it this way: it is the same amount of complexity, with no advantages. Using the explicit xhr or longpoll has a couple of small advantages. First it appears in the server logs, whereas HTTP headers usually do not. That might help troubleshooting. Second, there is the risk of a buggy browser forgetting to send the header, or missing out the hyphen, etc. Sending a URL parameter is fairly riskless.

So Is That Everything?

In this chapter we have looked at the `event:` feature of SSE as well as how it supports sending messages with multiple lines, plus how leading spaces can cause problems. We did not use any of these features in the FX application, because by using JSON they become unnecessary.

To answer the "So Is That Everything?" question: no, it is still not everything the SSE standard mentions. We still have CORS to talk about. This, along with authentication, will be covered in the next chapter.

CHAPTER 9

Authorization: Who's That Knocking at My Door?

In the previous chapters all our data push examples have been open to everyone. In this chapter I will show how we can limit access, whether by IP, cookie, or password. The good news is that it is as straightforward as protecting any other resource on your server.

But that is not the only topic of this chapter. There has been another restriction underlying all the examples in the earlier chapters, and the time has come to deal with that one, too. The restriction is that both your HTML file (that makes the SSE request and receives the data) and your server-side script (that sends the data) have had to reside on the same *server*. Well, server is too imprecise: they have to be in the same *origin*. Later in this chapter, we will look at the definition of an origin and then how to get around this restriction.

These two topics are closely related, but notice that they are orthogonal: your data push can fail because either you lack the authorization (IP, cookie, password) or because you come from a disallowed origin, or both. For data push to be successful, the client has to satisfy both.

If you are familiar with web applications and want the distilled version of this chapter, authentication and CORS mostly work just like they do for Ajax; but watch out for browser support and bugs.

This chapter will finish by taking the FX demo application from the earlier chapters and showing how to add authentication and CORS support to it.

Cookies

Cookies can be sent to an SSE script. The browser treats an SSE connection just the same as any other HTTP request when it comes to cookies, and you don't need to do anything. Here is a simple test frontend:

```
<html>
<head>
<title>Cookie logging test</title>
<script>
document.cookie="ssetest=123; path=/";
document.cookie="another-one=123; path=/";
</script>
</head>
<body>
<script>
var es = new EventSource('log_headers.php');
</script>
</body>
</html>
```

Of course those cookies could have been sent from another page on your website, not made in the JavaScript. This example reuses the logging script we looked at in "Headers" on page 123.

This example also works fine with all the fallbacks: XMLHttpRequests and iframe requests are treated just like any other HTTP request!

What about in the other direction: can the SSE server script send a cookie back? The answer is yes, as you can test with this pair of scripts. The frontend is trivial, no different from *basic_sse.html*, which we saw way back in Chapter 2:

```
<!doctype html>
<html>
  <head>
    <meta charset="UTF-8">
    <title>SSE: access count using cookies</title>
  </head>
  <body>
    <pre id="x">Initializing...</pre>
    <script>
    var es = new EventSource("sse_sending_cookies.php");
    es.addEventListener("message", function(e){
      document.getElementById("x").innerHTML += "\n" + e.data;
      },false);
    </script>
  </body>
</html>
```

That file is found as *sse_sending_cookies.html* in the book's code, and it is connecting to *sse_sending_cookies.php*, which is shown next. The backend code looks like *basic_sse.php*, but near the top it first looks for a cookie called "accessCount". (If not found, the @ suppresses the error, and the (int) cast will turn it into a zero.) It increments and sends back the new value. The new value is also shown in the output:

```php
<?php
header("Content-Type: text/event-stream");

$accessCount = (int)@$_COOKIE["accessCount"] + 1;
header("Set-Cookie: accessCount=".$accessCount);

while(true){
  echo "data:".$accessCount.":".date("Y-m-d H:i:s")."\n\n";
  @ob_flush();@flush();
  sleep(1);
  }
```

Now when you run the script you first see:

```
Initializing...
1:2014-02-28 14:17:33
1:2014-02-28 14:17:34
1:2014-02-28 14:17:35
...
```

Then if you press reload in your browser, it will instead show:

```
Initializing...
2:2014-02-28 14:17:40
2:2014-02-28 14:17:41
2:2014-02-28 14:17:42
...
```

Such fun!

Authorization (with Apache)

You can IP-restrict or password-protect any SSE script the same way you can protect any other URL. In the *.htaccess* file that comes with the book's source code, I have this block:

```
<Files "log_headers_ip_restrict.php">
  order deny,allow
  deny from all
  allow from 127.0.0.1
</Files>
```

It says that only browsers from localhost (127.0.0.1) are allowed access. Everyone else will be given a 403 error. Use *log_headers.ip_restrict.html* to test it: it just tries to connect, nothing else. (By the way, *log_headers_ip_restrict.php* is an exact copy of *log_head ers.php*, which we created in Chapter 8; the reason for duplicating it here is solely so we can apply these IP address restrictions on just that one file.)

If you are browsing from 127.0.0.1, you will get an entry in *tmp.log*. If you are browsing from anywhere else, there will be no entry in *tmp.log* (Apache would not even have started the PHP script). Browsers report the access denial in different ways. In the Firefox JavaScript console you will see something like "NetworkError: 403 Forbidden - http://example.com/log_headers_ip_restrict.php." In Chrome, go to the Network tab of the developer tools to see a canceled request.

As an aside, here is an alternative block that allows all the private IPv4 and IPv6 networks. I often find this one more useful:

```
<Files "log_headers_ip_restrict.php">
  order deny,allow
  deny from all
  allow from 127.0.0.1
  allow from 172.16.0.0/12
  allow from 10.0.0.0/8
  allow from 192.168.0.0/16
  allow from fc00::/7
</Files>
```

That was restricting access by something-you-are, an IP address. How about restricting access by something-you-know, i.e., with a username and password? I also have this block in the *.htaccess* file:

```
AuthUserFile /etc/apache2/sse_book_htpasswd
AuthType Basic
AuthName SSEBook
<Files "log_headers_basic_auth.php">
  require valid-user
</Files>
```

Actually in *.htaccess* you will find something like:

```
<Files ~ "^(log_headers_basic_auth[.]php|auth[.]basic_by_apache[.]php)$">
```

because it is also used by the script introduced in a later section. The tilde means it is regex, but in this case the regex is merely a list of alternatives, separated by vertical bars. The dots in filenames are matched exactly (rather than the regex meaning of a dot) by turning them into character classes (the square brackets).

I then have these contents in the */etc/apache2/sse_book_htpasswd* file:

```
oreilly:AhsbB/t5vHsxA
```

That is a basic auth password of "test" for the username "oreilly."

Use the `htpasswd` program to change to a different password. The password file can be anywhere on your disk—it does not have to be under the Apache configuration directory. Just change `AuthUser File` to match.

Now when you browse to *log_headers.basic_auth.html*, this sequence happens:

1. *log_headers.basic_auth.html* loads, because it is unprotected.
2. The JavaScript runs, and the `EventSource` object is created.
3. The browser connects to *log_headers_basic_auth.php*, and gets told by Apache that a username and password is needed.
4. The browser shows a dialog asking the user for that information.
5. The browser connects *again*, this time sending the username and password.
6. Apache verifies it and runs the PHP script.
7. The PHP script starts streaming data to the browser. (Though in this case, it logs headers then does not stream anything at all!)

Notice how the authentication is completely handled by Apache: the PHP script does not need to do anything, and knows it will not be started unless authentication has completed.

If your PHP script wants to double-check that Apache has been configured correctly and is asking for authentication, it should check that `REMOTE_USER` got set. *log_head ers basic auth.php* has this line at the very top:

```
if(!@$_SERVER["REMOTE_USER"])exit;
```

As subtle as a big, bad bouncer. Ain't got a pass? You can't come in.

 In PHP you can get the username of the person connecting with either `$_SERVER["REMOTE_USER"]` or `$_SERVER["PHP_AUTH_USER"]`. `$_SERV ER["PHP_AUTH_PW"]` is their password (in clear text). However, if PHP runs in safe mode, the `PHP_AUTH_*` values are not available.

HTTP POST with SSE

If you bought this book just to learn how to POST variables to an SSE backend, and you've turned straight to this section, I'd like you to take a deep breath, and make sure you are sitting down. You see, I have some bad news. How to break it to you gently... you remember as a child when you wanted to fly like Superman and everyone told you it couldn't be done, you'd never manage it, and they turned out to be right? Well, it is happening again.

The SSE standard has no way to allow you to POST data to the server. This is a very annoying oversight, and might get rectified at some point. After all, the XMLHttpRe quest object allows us to send POST data. (Ironically, that means we can easily send POST data for the fallback solutions introduced in Chapters 6 and 7.)

The reason I cover this in a chapter on authentication is that it is particularly annoying when it comes to doing a custom login. We do not want to send the username and password as GET data because it will be visible in the URL, will end up in server log files, and so on.

The SSE standard also does not let us specify HTTP headers, so using a custom header is out too. What to do?

Luckily there is one way to send non-URL data to an SSE process, and we looked at it at the start of this chapter: cookies! So, in your JavaScript, just before the call to new EventSource(), set a cookie something like this:

```
document.cookie = "login=oreilly,test;path=/";
```

(I know you already realize you are going to be doing something more dynamic than that, not hardcoding the username and password!) The password is in cleartext in your cookie. I strongly recommend that you only use this technique when also using SSL.

Then, over on the server side, here is how to handle the cookie data in PHP:

```php
<?php
if (!defined("PASSWORD_DEFAULT")) { //For 5.4.x and earlier
  function password_verify($password, $hash) {
  return crypt($password,$hash) === $hash;
  }
}   //End of if (!defined("PASSWORD_DEFAULT"))

$SSE = (@$_SERVER["HTTP_ACCEPT"] == "text/event-stream");
if($SSE)header("Content-Type: text/event-stream");
else header("Content-Type: text/plain");

if(!array_key_exists("login", $_COOKIE)){
    echo "data: The login cookie is missing. Exiting.\n\n";
    exit;
    }
list($user, $pw) = explode(",", $_COOKIE["login"]);

$fromDB = '$2a$10$4LLeBta770Y0Z7795j.8'.
  'He/ZCQonnvImXIX0egalzE1MuWiEa6PQa';

if(!password_verify($pw, $fromDB)){
  echo "data: The login cookie is bad. Exiting.\n\n";
  exit;
```

```
    }
  while(true){
    echo "data:".date("Y-m-d H:i:s")."\n\n";
    @ob_flush();@flush();
    sleep(1);
    }
  }
```

(That is the full code for *auth.custom.php*, which we will be using in the next section.)

The SSE header is done first, so that login error messages can be sent just like any other data. Then explode() turns a CSV string (our cookie) into an array, and list($user, $pw) turns that array into two variables. $fromDB is a hardcoded string here, but, as the name suggests, this would normally come from an SQL query to get the hashed password. Then the password is hashed and validated using password_verify() and if it does not match what was found in the database, access is denied.

 The hardcoded password shown in the preceding code listing was generated with password_hash(), which, along with password_ver ify(), was added in PHP 5.5 to encourage best practices for password security. They are easy to write in earlier versions of PHP, and the code for that is shown in "Passwords" on page 199. (So the preceding listing can be used out of the box in earlier versions; pass word_verify() has been defined inline.)

By the way, that login cookie will be sent to all pages on our site, because path was specified as /, which is likely to be undesirable. If so, in your production system, make the SSE server URL look like a path (e.g., use Apache's mod_rewrite) and then set the cookie path to be that.

Also, we set the *document* cookie. That means it is tied to the domain name we loaded the HTML from. When we look at CORS later in this chapter, this will mean that if we have to connect to a different backend, we cannot send a cookie to that backend. So this "cookie-instead-of-POST" hack can only be used when the HTML file and the SSE backend are on the same server.

Multiple Authentication Choices

The following example file, *auth_test.html*, offers the user three ways to log in to the site. The first is by giving the values in an HTML form. (I have them filled in already to ease testing—don't do this in production!) This puts them in a cookie and submits them to the *auth.custom.php* script that was shown in the previous section. The other two buttons will use HTTP basic authorization. The first has Apache do the authorization, and the second has PHP do it. We have already looked at how Apache authorization works, controlled by the *.htaccess* file.

The way to do basic authorization directly in PHP looks a bit like the cookie example shown in the previous section, but we get the login details from PHP_AUTH_USER and PHP_AUTH_PW. Here is the extract from *auth.basic_by_php.php* that handles the authentication:

```
$user = @$_SERVER["PHP_AUTH_USER"];
$pw = @$_SERVER["PHP_AUTH_PW"];

$fromDB = '$2a$10$4LLeBta770Y0Z7795j.8'.
  'He/ZCQonnvImXIX0egalzE1MuWiEa6PQa';
if(!password_verify($pw,$fromDB)){
  header('WWW-Authenticate: Basic realm="SSE Book"');
  header("HTTP/1.0 401 Unauthorized");
  echo "Please authenticate.\n";
  exit;
}
```

When authentication fails, those HTTP headers are sent back to the browser. These are what cause the browser to prompt the user with a login dialog box.

Here is the full *auth_test.html* code. It is an interesting study because it also shows how to create a delayed EventSource connection, only on demand. In contrast, practically all our previous examples have done the connection automatically when first loaded.

```
<!doctype html>
<html>
  <head>
    <title>SSE: Basic/Custom Auth Test</title>
    <meta charset="UTF-8">
    <script>
    var es = null;

    function formSubmit(form){
    document.cookie = "login="
      + form.username.value
      + "," + form.password.value
      + "; path=/";
    startSSE("auth.custom.php");
    }

    function authByApache(){
    startSSE("auth.basic_by_apache.php");
    }

    function authByPHP(){
    startSSE("auth.basic_by_php.php");
    }

    function startSSE(url){
    document.getElementById("x").innerHTML = "";
    if(es){
      document.getElementById("x").innerHTML
```

```
            += "Closing connection.\n";
        es.close();
        }
    document.getElementById("x").innerHTML
        += "Connecting to " + url +"\n";
    es = new EventSource(url);
    es.addEventListener("message", function(e){
        document.getElementById("x").innerHTML += "\n" + e.data;
        },false);
    }
    </script>
</head>
<body>
    <div style="float:right">
    <form action="" onSubmit="formSubmit(this);return false">
    Username: <input type="text" name="username" id="username" value="oreilly" />
    <br/>
    Password: <input type="password" name="password" value="test" />
    <br/>
    <input type="submit" value="Submit these credentials to auth.custom.php"/>
    </form>
    <br/>
    <button onClick="authByApache()">Use auth.basic_by_apache.php</button>
    <br/>
    <button onClick="authByPHP()">Use auth.basic_by_php.php</button>
    </div>
    <pre id="x">Waiting...</pre>
</body>
</html>
```

SSL and CORS (Connecting to Other Servers)

First the good news. You can use SSE (and all the fallbacks discussed in this book) on either an HTTP server or an HTTPS server. When the HTML file is downloaded from an HTTP server, it wants to connect to get data from an HTTP server. When downloaded from an HTTPS server, it wants to get data from an HTTPS server.[1]

If you try to connect to an HTTPS server from a page downloaded from HTTP, or vice versa, you get the "The connection to ... was interrupted while the page was loading." error in Firefox. Chrome is barely any better: "Uncaught Error: SecurityError: DOM Exception 18." Other browsers will tell you something equally obscure. In fact, they are all complaining about a CORS failure. Read on.

---

[1]. In Chrome at the time of writing, EventSource will not work with a self-signed SSL certificate, nor will any of the fallbacks.

If you intend to follow along in the next few sections with Chrome or Safari, make sure you have at least Chromium 26 or Safari 7, because CORS support was missing or buggy until then. Firefox support has been fine since much earlier. See "Chrome and Safari and CORS" on page 150.

CORS stands for Cross-Origin Resource Sharing. I wonder if they started with a catchy abbreviation then tried to find some words to fit. Anyway, CORS is the solution for the Same-Origin Policy. The Same-Origin Policy is a security feature: if you download an HTML file from a server, your browser will only let you connect back to that exact same server. (This is not specific to SSE; it affects your Ajax connections and web font requests, too.)

That is a shame, isn't it? What if AcmeFeeds wants to sell a weather data feed, hosted at *weather.example.com*, and wants its clients to be able to put a little JavaScript widget on their own websites that will connect to *weather.example.com*? The Same-Origin Policy says this is not allowed.

Here is an alternative viewpoint. What if AcmeWeather has a weather data feed hosted at *weather.example.com*, and it runs a website, also at *weather.example.com*, that uses advertising to pay for the costs of maintaining the data feed? AcmeWeather doesn't want some other sneaky website stealing just its data feed, for which it will get no advertising revenue.

The browser's default state is to protect AcmeWeather: browsers do not allow someone to consume data from another website. And so CORS was invented to allow AcmeFeeds to override that default and tell the world that it is OK to take its data.

Basically, CORS is the way for a server to say it is OK to relax the Same-Origin Policy. If you have used CORS with the `XMLHttpRequest` object (i.e., with Ajax), you will be happy to know that the `EventSource` object works in basically the same way.

So, what exactly is an origin? Two resources are in the same origin if:

- Their hostnames match (e.g., "example.com" and "somethingelse.com" are different, "www1.example.com" and "www2.example.com" are different, "10.1.2.3" and "example.com" are different even if "example.com" resolves to 10.1.2.3).
- Their schemes match (e.g., both *http://* or both *https://*).
- Their ports match (e.g., "http://example.com:80" and "http://example.com:8080" are different origins, but "http://example.com" and "http://example.com:80" are the same origin).

See *http://tools.ietf.org/html/rfc6454#section-4* if you need a more precise definition. See *http://www.w3.org/TR/cors/* for all the gory details on CORS.

CORS is implemented by the SSE server-side script sending back extra headers to say what it allows. That is what we will look at next.

Allow-Origin

To try this out, add this line near the top of your server script:

```
header("Access-Control-Allow-Origin: *");
```

This line says: "Anyone browsing from anywhere is allowed to receive data from this server script." It has been added to *fx_server.cors.php*, which is otherwise just a copy of the FX application demo server script, as of the end of Chapter 7. See the following sidebar for how to test that this header is having the desired effect.

Testing CORS

Testing requires a bit more setup than in previous examples. You need to serve the HTML from one origin and have it connect to an SSE server in another origin, meaning a different hostname and/or a different port and/or a different protocol. However, this does not need two machines, just a bit of web server configuration. If you don't know how to do that, a web search should bring up plenty of tutorials for your OS and web server combination.

To allow us to test CORS, I have created *fx_client.cors.html*, which connects to *fx_server.cors.php*. However, *fx_client.cors.html* is one of the few listings in the book's source code that might not be usable out of the box, depending on how you have set up your servers. Instead of this line:

```
var url = "fx_server.cors.php?";
```

you will find:

```
var url = window.location.href.replace(
    "fx_client.cors.html","fx_server.cors.php?");
```

It is making an absolute URL instead of a relative one. So if you were hosting this project at *http://www.example.com/oreilly/sse/listings/fx_client.cors.html*, it would set url to *http://www.example.com/oreilly/sse/listings/***fx_server.cors.php?**.

Next we have:

```
if(url.indexOf("https") >= 0)
    url = url.replace("https://","http://");
else url = url.replace("http://","https://");
```

These lines swap between HTTP and HTTPS. To support this I set up Apache SSL, with a self-signed certificate, but on the same IP address and pointing to the same Document Root. So when I browse to *http://www.example.com/oreilly/sse/listings/fx_client.cors.html*, it connects to ***https:**//www.example.com/oreilly/sse/listings/fx_server.cors.php?* and

---

when I browse to *https://www.example.com/oreilly/sse/listings/fx_client.cors.html*, it con-nects to ***http://www.example.com/oreilly/sse/listings/fx_server.cors.php?***.

After that we have a way to test origins that are different in the hostname part:

```
url = url.replace("//www1.","//www.");
```

When I browse to *www1.example.com* it will instead connect to *www.example.com*. When I browse to *www.example.com*, or anything other than *www1*, it does nothing, and so will continue to connect to that same domain.

I configured Apache to handle all of the above by duplicating the *www.example.com* virtual host, in both HTTP and HTTPS, and calling it *example1.com*. So, when I browse to *http://www1.example.com/oreilly/sse/listings/fx_client.cors.html* it connects to *https://www.example.com/oreilly/sse/listings/fx_server.cors.php?*.

When testing, it is often easier to just add an another IP address, rather than add another hostname. Here is a way to convert an IP address in a URL:

```
url = url.replace(
  /([/][/]\d+[.]\d+[.]\d+)[.]51[/]/,
  "$1.50/");
```

Vicious regex. Simply put, it changes a final IP address component of "51" to "50," so if I browse to *http://10.0.0.51/oreilly/sse/listings/fx_client.cors.html* it connects to ***https://10.0.0.50/oreilly/sse/listings/fx_server.cors.php?***.

The final addition is to report the changes it made; this is just for troubleshooting pur-poses:

```
console.log("Our URL is "
  + window.location.href
  + "; connecting to " + url);
```

Now, to convince yourself it is actually working, first browse to *fx_server.cors.html* with both *http://* and *https://* on a couple of different domain names. It should work. Then edit *fx_server.cors.php* to comment out header("Access-Control-Allow-Origin: *"); and all those variations should stop working.

Fine Access Control

The * in header("Access-Control-Allow-Origin: *"); opens it up to every Tom, Dick, and Harry. Luckily, finer control is possible. So, for example, try changing it to this: header("Access-Control-Allow-Origin: http://www.example.com"); (the http:// prefix is required). Now when you browse to *http://www.example.com/oreilly/sse/listings/fx_client.cors.html*, it connects to *https://www.example.com/oreilly/sse/listings/fx_server.cors.php?* and it works. But, as we learned at the start of this chapter, browsing from any of these will fail:

- **https://**_www.example.com/…/fx_client.cors.html_
- _http://_**www1**_.example.com/…/fx_client.cors.html_
- _http://www.example.com:_**88**_/…/fx_client.cors.html_
- _http://_**some.other.domain.com**_/…/fx_client.cors.html_

 `Access-Control-Allow-Origin` is not a substitute for proper authentication: a client can forge the `Origin` header. Also remember that you are reliant on the browser to implement CORS correctly.

CORS is not as flexible as you might want. You can use "*" for everything, or you can specify exactly _one_ origin, i.e., exactly one combination of HTTP versus HTTPS, domain, and port. Two choices: one origin or every origin. For anything in between, you have to parse the `Origin` header in your script. Here is the most basic example, which is actually identical to using `"Access-Control-Allow-Origin: *"`:[2]

```
header("Access-Control-Allow-Origin: ".@$_SERVER['HTTP_ORIGIN']);
```

(The @ sign means suppress errors, so if `HTTP_ORIGIN` is not set, it will quietly evaluate to the empty string; in this case that would mean CORS would then always cause the connection to be refused.)

Here is a more interesting example:

```
if(preg_match('|https?://www[1-6]\.example\.com$|',@$_SERVER["HTTP_ORIGIN"]))
    header("Access-Control-Allow-Origin: ".$_SERVER["HTTP_ORIGIN"]);
else header("Access-Control-Allow-Origin: http://www.example.com");
```

Starting from the final line, if the regex does not match, it says you have to be browsing from _http://www.example.com_. I talk about regexes in "Comparing Two URLs" on page 157, but this one is relatively simple: it says any of _wwwN.example.com_ will match (where N is 1, 2, 3, 4, 5, or 6), and will be told it is OK to connect. I also explicitly allow both HTTP and HTTPS URLs (the question mark after "s" means the "s" is optional). Take note that _**https**://www.example.com_ will fail to match because it is not any of _www1_ to _www6_; put a ? after the [1-6] to have that be optional, too.

Don't you feel we could do a bit better than this? Your goal was to say only clients who downloaded our application HTML from _www.example.com, www1.example.com_, etc., are allowed to connect. No one else is. How about we write that goal more explicitly:

---

2. Did I say identical? There is a key difference when it comes to using credentials. See "Constructors and Credentials" on page 151.

```
if(preg_match('|https?://www[1-6]?\.example\.com$|',@$_SERVER["HTTP_ORIGIN"]))
    header("Access-Control-Allow-Origin: ".$_SERVER["HTTP_ORIGIN"]);
else{
  header("HTTP/1.1 403 Forbidden");
  exit;
  }
```

I fiddled with the regex so it covers *www.example.com* (and therefore allows both HTTP and HTTPS for that subdomain) too. But when anyone else is trying to connect, it dies immediately. I would put this code near the top of the server script.

HEAD and OPTIONS

So far we have only considered that the browser might send GET or POST requests. It would be weird of them to send something else, such as PUT, when requesting a stream of new data. In PHP, at least, all request methods are treated identically. If a client sent a HEAD request our code would behave badly: it is not supposed to send any body, and in fact we would not just be sending content but would keep the connection open forever. One option is to return from a HEAD request, just before entering the main loop (i.e., after all headers have been sent). But another approach is to decide HEAD requests are silly, and not accept them. To do this, the following code can go at the very top of the script:

```
switch($_SERVER["REQUEST_METHOD"]){
  case "GET":case "POST":break;
  case "OPTIONS":break;  //TODO
  default:
    header("HTTP/1.0 405 Method Not Allowed");
    header("Allow: GET,POST,OPTIONS");
    exit;
    }
  }
```

This HTTP method checking is not really related to the topic of this chapter, which is authentication and CORS. It is being discussed now to prepare the way for handling OPTIONS (coming up next).

If you felt the need, then for the examples in earlier chapters, where only GET makes sense, you could do it more simply by putting this at the top of your script:

```
if($_SERVER['REQUEST_METHOD']!='GET')↵
{header("HTTP/1.0 405 Method Not Allowed");header("Allow: GET");exit;}
```

The Allow header is required when sending back a 405, and it specifies what headers are allowed. What is that reference to OPTIONS though?

The idea is that a browser can call your script with an OPTIONS method to get back information on what parts of the HTTP protocol are supported. In the context of CORS, this is called a *preflight* request, and is typically used to ask what information is allowed to be sent to the origin in question.

 If using Apache authentication, note that the OPTIONS request will be failed with a 401 ("Authorization required"), and never actually reach your script. The browser should then prompt the user to authenticate, but some browsers (e.g., Safari 5.1) do not.

Annoyingly, sending back a wildcard for the `"Access-Control-Allow-Headers"` response does not seem to work, so you have to waste bandwidth trying to guess every header a browser might want to send. Here is one way to implement it:

```
...
case "OPTIONS":
  header("Access-Control-Allow-Origin: *");
  header("Access-Control-Allow-Headers: Last-Event-ID,".
    " Origin, X-Requested-With, Content-Type, Accept,".
    " Authorization");
  exit;
```

To do the same thing in Node.js, the idea is similar. However, POST handling in Node.js is a bit complicated, so it uses two dedicated functions (not shown) to handle each of GET and POST, and the request handler is completely replaced by this switch function:

```
function(request,response){
  switch(request.method){
    case "GET":handleGET(request,response);break;
    case "POST":handlePOST(request,response);break;
    case "OPTIONS":
      response.writeHead(200,{
        "Access-Control-Allow-Origin: *",
        "Access-Control-Allow-Headers: Last-Event-ID," +
        " Origin, X-Requested-With, Content-Type, Accept," +
        " Authorization"
        });
      break;
    default:
      response.writeHead(405,{
        "Allow: GET,POST,OPTIONS"
        });
      break;
  }
}
```

Chrome and Safari and CORS

Webkit-based browsers have/had some bugs that stop CORS from working correctly with native SSE. The CORS implementation of `EventSource` was broken/missing in Chrome 25 and earlier, and Safari 6 and earlier. As I type these words most people are now past Chrome 25, but quite a few people are still using Safari 6. If that was the bad news, the even worse news is that it is well-nigh impossible to use feature detection for this.

If CORS is an essential part of your system, the workaround is to force Chrome and Safari to use XHR instead of SSE. Sounds horrible, doesn't it? However, it is not quite that bad, because bandwidth-wise and connection-wise, XHR is almost as good as SSE. There are really only two downsides to XHR compared to SSE:

- Writing the extra code for both SSE and XHR support: but we have already done that.
- Having to reconnect when memory gets too big. See "Thanks for the Memories" on page 119 in Chapter 7.

The example at the end of this chapter uses browser version detection to tell older versions of Chrome and Safari to use XHR instead of native SSE. As it just does some regexes, it is not shown in this book, so if you are interested, take a look at `function oldSafariChromeDetect()` in *fx_client.auth.html* in the book's source code.

Chrome has another problem, though it is one that will only come up during development and testing: self-signed SSL certificates get rejected. This happens with both XHR and SSE, and the `--disable-web-security` command-line flag does not help. So, it is not a problem specific to Chrome's SSE implementation. In fact, this bug is not even specific to CORS—you cannot connect with `XMLHttpRequest` or `EventSource` to a self-signed HTTPS server, period.[3] You can work around it by adding your server certificate to the Trusted Root Certificates on your local machine. Or wait for the developers to fix it. Or, because self-signed certificates are normally just used when testing and developing, develop using Firefox and other browsers and only test with Chrome when it goes on your production server.

iOS7 works with CORS and native SSE, but when connecting to an SSE data source that requests authentication, there is no dialog prompt for the password. XHR has the same problem, so we cannot work around it. If you want to support iPhone/iPad, you will have to arrange for users to access a page on your target server directly, so that they can be prompted to give the username and password. The browser will then hold on to those

---

3. You can follow the bug report at *http://code.google.com/p/chromium/issues/detail?id=96007*.

credentials, and they will be sent when the SSE or Ajax connection is made. (The cookie approach to authentication does not have this issue.)

Constructors and Credentials

You must know by now that the `EventSource` constructor takes the URL parameter to connect to. It turns out that there is a second parameter, which takes an object containing options. At the current time there is just one possible option, `withCredentials`, which is Boolean and defaults to `false`.

Try setting it to `true` on any of the earlier FX application code. Change this line:

```
es = new EventSource(u);
```

to this line:

```
es = new EventSource(u, { withCredentials: true } );
```

If you are connecting to the same server, it has no effect. But do the same change in our CORS version, and try to connect to a different protocol, host, or port. It breaks. In Firefox you get told "The connection was interrupted."

We fix it by having the server-side script send these two headers *instead* of `header("Access-Control-Allow-Origin: *");`:

```
header("Access-Control-Allow-Origin: ".@$_SERVER["HTTP_ORIGIN"]);
header("Access-Control-Allow-Credentials: true");
```

The second of those headers says, "Yes, we are happy for you to send credentials." But this header is not allowed to be used with `"Access-Control-Allow-Origin: *"`. The browser thinks we are being a bit too promiscuous. So, do you remember that line we said earlier that was equivalent to `"Access-Control-Allow-Origin: *"`? That is perfect for here. It does exactly the same thing, but makes the browser go, "Ooooh, this server has obviously listened to the lecture on safe intercourse, so let's believe it when it also says it wants to allow credentials."

Get up and do a happy dance, because with those two lines the client can now add the `withCredentials:true` option, and everything works again. But just what is it we've allowed to happen?!

withCredentials

Say you get your HTML from *http://example.com/index.html*, and it tries to make an SSE connection to *http://www1.example.com/sse.php*. If you have made it this far in this chapter, you must know that will fail due to the Same-Origin Policy. And you know that by having the server set a `"Access-Control-Allow-Origin:"` that is either * or your client's origin, the Same-Origin Policy will be overridden, and the connection will work.

You also know, if you've been following along, that HTTP authentication works fine with SSE.

The problem comes when we try to combine these two things. By default, when you access another origin it won't send along the HTTP headers needed for authentication. If the SSE server script (or Apache) sends back a 401 (which would normally trigger showing the user the dialog to input his name and password), it will just be treated as an error.

 Earlier we used cookies to implement a custom login system, in lieu of POST not being supported by `EventSource`. `withCredentials` does also mean cookies can be sent, but it is no use to us here because we can only set a cookie on *document*, which means we are setting it on our *origin*, and cookies registered for one IP address or hostname cannot be sent to a different IP address or hostname.

What does that mean? It means we cannot use native SSE with a custom login system if we need to connect to a different origin. Simply Not Possible.[4]

The solution? Hope that a future version of the SSE standard will allow POST data. The hack? In the example you will find at the end of this chapter, we detect when one is trying to do custom authentication to a different origin, and force the connection to fall back to use XHR instead of SSE. Or use basic authentication. Or avoid using different origins. Or use out-of-bound authentication, so a cookie for the SSE server is received before trying to open the SSE connection.

So, to get around this the client needs to pass `{ withCredentials: true }` as the second parameter to the `EventSource` constructor, as shown in the previous section, and the server needs to send back the `"Access-Control-Allow-Credentials"` header, set to `true`, as well as set the `"Access-Control-Allow-Origin"` header to whatever origin the client specified. Once you do that, HTTP authentication (and cookies[5]) work with CORS.

Well, they work in a *modern* browser. And XHR works in exactly the same way, so they work with our fallbacks. Well, kind of…see the next section.

---

4. Well, not quite. In Firefox, at least, you can send cookies from *http://example.com* to *https://example.com*, and vice versa (i.e., origins that differ in just the scheme part). My suggestion is not to rely on this behavior, because it is inconsistent with the CORS/cookies behavior of XHR and therefore might change in the future.

5. Those that are allowed to be sent. Other cookies still apply so, for instance, a cookie for *www1.example.com* cannot be sent to *www2.example.com*.

A reminder, once again, that none of this is *real* security. It all relies on the client obeying the rules. With a few lines of code in your scripting language of choice, or a curl one-liner, you can send auth headers, cookies, GET data, POST data, and even a picture of Her Majesty Queen Elizabeth II to any SSE server, whether they send you Access-Control- headers or not. While at it, you may as well also forge the User-Agent header, and the Origin header.

CORS, and withCredentials, are mainly there to prevent Cross-Site Request Forgery (CSRF) (*http://en.wikipedia.org/wiki/CSRF*) and similar attacks.

CORS and Fallbacks

Throughout this book I have tried to achieve 99% browser coverage, by showing SSE equivalents that work practically as well for older browsers. The good news is that CORS is available in XHR[6] and works exactly the same way. Therefore, because they use XMLHttpRequest, you don't need to do anything differently for the long-poll or XHR techniques that we studied in Chapters 6 and 7. IE9 and earlier are a problem, however.

But before we look at IE8/IE9, let's add CORS support to XHR for the browsers that support it. OK, done that. Yes, it was quick and easy because CORS is done entirely with the server headers; nothing changes in the JavaScript API.

But that is CORS without credentials support. For instance, our FX demo application sends a custom header (Last-Event-ID). So, you must use withCredentials, not just plain CORS. Let's add withCredentials to XHR for browsers that support it. This requires changing the startXHR() function:

```
function startXHR(){
...
xhr = new XMLHttpRequest();
...
xhr.open("GET", u, true);
if(lastId)xhr.setRequestHeader("Last-Event-ID", lastId);
xhr.send(null);
}
```

Instead of the options object that we saw with SSE's EventSource constructor, for XHR you set the third parameter to be true.

Next, we do the same change in the startLongPoll function:

---

6. Firefox has supported CORS with XHR since 3.5, Chrome since 4.0, Safari since 4.0, IE since either 8.0 or 10.0 depending on the level of support, and iOS Safari and Android since 3.2 and 2.1, respectively. In other words, excepting Internet Explorer, all your users can be assumed to have CORS support for XMLHttpRe quest.

```
function startLongPoll(){
...
if(window.XMLHttpRequest)xhr = new XMLHttpRequest();
else{
  document.getElementById("msg").innerHTML +=
    "** Your browser does not support XMLHttpRequest. Sorry.**<br>";
  }
...
if ("withCredentials" in xhr){
  xhr.open("GET", u, true);
  }else{
  document.getElementById("msg").innerHTML +=
    "** Your browser does not support CORS. Sorry.**<br>";
  }

if(lastId)xhr.setRequestHeader("Last-Event-ID", lastId);
xhr.send(null);
}
```

As well as setting the third parameter of open() to be true, I also stripped out the code for doing Ajax in IE6/7, and give an error message instead. That is IE6/7 taken care of, then further down we check for withCredentials support, and if it is not available (i.e., IE8/9), we report it as an error (we'll take care of that in the next section).

(You can find the preceding version in the book's source code as *fx_client.cors_xhr.html*.)

I could have done the same checks in startXHR(). I don't bother because the code in connect() is already making sure IE9 and earlier don't get there. I've not found a browser that ends up in startXHR() but does not support CORS and credentials; if you find one, please let me know.

CORS and IE9 and Earlier

I said long-poll and XHR techniques are fine. The iframe technique introduced in Chapter 7 is a different matter. It won't work. For security reasons, one iframe cannot access iframe content that came from a different domain. And there is no CORS-like workaround that we can use to say it is OK. So, what that means is that IE8 and IE9 will have to use long-poll if different domains are a possibility in your application.

If you just said, "What about IE6 or IE7?" you are asking too much: they do not have a CORS mechanism we can use, even with XHR (i.e., long-poll). So, IE7 and earlier simply cannot be made to work with different origins. You have to host the HTML and data push server on the same origin.

Do you need to use `withCredentials`, too? That is, do you need to send either auth headers or cookies to a server in a different origin, and have it work with IE8/IE9? Sorry, that is one requirement too far. The problem is that IE8 and IE9's CORS equivalent, called `XDomainRequest`, explicitly refuses to send any custom headers (including auth headers) and explicitly refuses to send cookies. If you *must* have authentication and you *must* support IE8/IE9, then you *have to* serve the HTML page and the SSE server from the same origin. (Use a load balancer or reverse proxy that will have all your servers on the same domain name, and use some other way to specify any differences between them.)

 IE10 and later already use the XHR technique, and CORS works for them. And `withCredentials` works too! Nothing needs to change for IE10 and later.

`XDomainRequest` is more restrictive[7] than real CORS. The "only GET or POST" restriction does not affect us, nor does the restriction that the MIME type must be `text/plain`. But there is one difference you need to watch out for: different schemes are never allowed. That means an HTML page served from *http://example.com* cannot access a server on *https://example.com*, and vice versa. There is no way for our server to say it is fine.

Here is how the code in `startLongPoll()` has to change to use `XDomainRequest` so that CORS will work for IE8 and IE9:

```
if ("withCredentials" in xhr){
  xhr.open("GET", u, true);
  }else if (typeof XDomainRequest != "undefined") {
  xhr = new XDomainRequest();
  xhr.open("GET", u);
  }else{
  document.getElementById("msg").innerHTML +=
    "** Your browser does not support CORS. Sorry.**<br>";
  }
xhr.onreadystatechange = longPollOnReadyStateChange;
```

As you can see, `XDomainRequest` is a drop-in replacement for `XMLHttpRequest`. However, the way we do feature detection means we cannot see if we need it until after creating the `XMLHttpRequest` object. Because `xhr` might get created again, we cannot do anything with it until after this block. That is why the assignment to `xhr.onready statechange` has been moved to after this block.

---

7. See *http://bit.ly/1csbEHT* for how it works in IE8 and IE9. Note that only GET or POST are allowed, cookies are not sent, and it must be `text/plain`.

The next two sections will show two different ways to handle using `startLongPoll()` with IE9 and earlier.

IE8/IE9: Always Use Long-Poll

If you know for sure that you are always dealing with different origins, it is easy: in `connect()`, change this block of code:

```
...
else if(isIE9OrEarlier){
  if(window.postMessage)startIframe();
  else startLongPoll();
  }
...
```

to this:

```
...
else if(isIE9OrEarlier){
  startLongPoll();
  }
...
```

As a bonus you can now also rip out the iframe code. Meaning, these can go:

- All of `function startIframe()`
- A couple of clauses in `function disconnect()`
- `var iframe` and `var iframeTimer`

Handling IE9 and Earlier Dynamically

What about when you do not know if you will hit the security restriction? It could be that this is library code that will be used on multiple sites. Or perhaps it is simply that the URL is sent to the browser client dynamically, and it is not known if you will be connecting to the same server or a different one.[8] In that case, change the previous code to look like this:

```
...
else if(is_ie_9_or_earlier){
  if(window.postMessage && isSameDomain())
    start_iframe();
  else start_longpoll();
  }
...
```

---

8. I find this "URL is sent to the browser client dynamically" scenario a bit of a stretch. In such a case it sounds like you would mostly be connecting to another server. If so, simplify the code to always use long-poll.

I have hidden all the extra logic in the isSameDomain() function.[9] What does the isSameDomain() function have to do? It has to compare url with window.location.href, and return true if all these are the same:

- The protocol (HTTP versus HTTPS)
- The server name (or IP address)
- The port

There are two ways to write this. One uses regexes. The other uses a cute little JavaScript +DOM trick. You will see both ways described in the following sidebar. (In the book's source code, *fx_client.cors_xhr_ie.html* implements both ways, but uses the regex approach.)

Comparing Two URLs

Whenever we need to compare multiple parts of two strings, regexes are the tool for the job. If you've been resisting learning regexes because they look utterly unreadable, just give in. You can do so much merely knowing the basic syntax.

As an aside, whatever your regex skill level, you might find using this tester tool helpful as you follow along with the explanation: *http://www.regexplanet.com/advanced/java script/index.html*.

Here is the regex to extract the protocol, server name, and port from a URL:

```
/^(https?):[/][/]([^/:]+)(:([^/]+))?/
```

The / on either side mark the start and end of the regex. The ^ means this has to match at the start of the string. Parentheses surround something we want to capture, and there are three blocks of capturing going on here, shown highlighted here:

```
/^(https?):[/][/]([^/:]+)(:([^/]+))?/
```

The first string to capture is the scheme (HTTP or HTTPS), second is the domain name, and third is the optional port number. The ? after the parentheses means zero or once, so if there is no port number, the third captured string will simply be undefined. The second block, [^/:]+, says grab everything until reaching either a forward slash or a colon (the slash or colon will not be part of the captured string). The next one, [^/]+, says grab everything until reaching a forward slash. In both cases the end of the string would also terminate the capturing. (There are also another pair of parentheses, which are being used for grouping, not for capturing. Their purpose in life is to make sure the colon prefix is not part of the port number that is captured.)

---

9. This function will make an appearance again, in the final example in this chapter, when deciding whether to use SSE-with-cookies or having to fallback to XHR so that POST data can be sent.

Between the protocol and the domain name comes `://`. Why the funny notation (`:[/]`
`[/]`)? The forward slash symbol is already being used to mark the start and end of the
regex, so forward slashes need to be escaped if used anywhere else. But, they *don't* need
to be escaped in character classes. Square brackets mark character classes. So `[/]` is the
same as writing `\/`, and both mean match one forward slash. I personally think the
character class approach is clearer (especially when putting the regex in a string where
backslashes need to be escaped: then the forward slash can end up looking like `\\/` or
even `\\\\/`).

Defining the regex between `/.../` implicitly creates a `RegExp`
object. You could also create it explicitly with `var re = new`
`RegExp('^(https?)://([^/:]+)(:([^/]+))?');`. These approaches are identical. Note that in the second way, "/" is no
longer used to start and end the regex, so it no longer needs to
be escaped! So I can use "/" characters directly and not have to
write them as `[/]`.

I could also have not assigned the regex to the `re` variable, and
merged the first two lines into one: `var m1 = /^(https?):[/]`
`[/]([^/:]+)(:([^/]+))?/.exec( url )`.

That is a bad idea for *two* reasons, *both* reasons being that I use
the regex twice. The first reason is the obvious one of duplicate
code being A Bad Thing™. The second reason is that by assigning a regex to a variable, it gets compiled. Because we use that
compiled regex twice, we save ourselves the CPU effort of one
extra regex compilation. Here that is minor. It matters more if the
regex is inside a 1,000-iteration loop. But, on principle, always
assign your regexes to a variable if using them more than once.
Going further with that idea, if a regex is being called a lot, for
instance every time the server sends us data, then I would be
tempted to assign the regex to a *global* variable, so it is only
compiled once in the whole script.

Turning all that chat into JavaScript code, here is what we get:

```
function isSameDomain(){
var re = /^(https?):[/][/]([^/:]+)(:([^/]+))?/;
var m1 = re.exec( url );
if(!m1)return true;
var m2 = re.exec( window.location.href );
if(m1[1] != m2[1])return false;
if(m1[2] != m2[2])return false;
if(m1[4] != m2[4]){
    if(!m1[4])m1[4] = (m1[1]=='http') ? "80" : "443";
    if(!m2[4])m2[4] = (m2[1]=='http') ? "80" : "443";
    if(m1[4] != m2[4])return false;
    }
```

```
    return true;
}
```

`exec` called on a `RegExp` object gives an array of matches. [1] is the first match (protocol), [2] is the second match (server name), and [4] is the port number ([3] is the port number including the colon, and is not used here). The port number needs a couple of extra lines of code, because if one version contains the default port number and the other left it off, we want them to match. That is, *http://example.com/* and *http://example.com: 80/* are the same thing. (If you ever find a browser that treats them differently, file a bug report and then add a hack to not execute those two lines for that browser!)

The regex fails if the URL is a relative URL. In other words, instead of *http://example.com/fx_server.php*, it is */fx_server.php*. It turns out that this is a solution, not a problem: relative URLs must be the same origin, by definition! So, if the regex does not match, assume it is a relative URL, and return true immediately. That is what the `if(!m1)return true;` line is doing.

This assumes you never have genuinely bad values for `url`. But that should be under the control of your application. And, anyway, the worst that happens is that with a bad URL, IE8 will try to use iframe and fail (for a security reason) instead of using long-poll and failing (because the URL is bad).

The regex also fails with "//example.com/..." style URLs, which are intended to use the same protocol (allowing code to be shared between HTTP and HTTPS sites). I chose not to complicate the regex even further by handling this. It is better to have two or three understandable regexes than one monster that covers all cases. To get you started, the regex you seek is `/^([/][/])([^/:] +)(:([^/]+))?/`. The *fx_client.cors_xhr_ie.html* file implements it fully.

I said there was another way to do this. Let me go straight into some code:

```
function isSameDomain(){
var m1 = document.createElement("a");
m1.href = url;
var m2 = document.createElement("a");
m2.href = window.location.href;
if(m1.protocol != m2.protocol)return false;
if(m1.hostname != m2.hostname)return false;
if(m1.port != m2.port)return false;
return true;
}
```

This relies on the fact that when JavaScript creates an <a> tag in the DOM, it will get a full `Location` object, which has all these lovely fields ready for you. And not a regex in sight. So cool. The downsides are that it is a bit more fragile, it is not available in IE6 or IE7, and there may be other small browser differences. You also need to test how it works in all the browsers where it will be used for the corner cases we had to deal with in the earlier code (relative URLs, "//example.com/" URLs, port number explicit in one but not in the other, etc.).

 I learned the technique at *https://gist.github.com/jlong/2428561*, though it was apparently discovered earlier than that. The comments on that page are also educational.

Putting It All Together

Did the last couple of sections make your head hurt, your eyes water, and mountain shepherd start to look like an attractive career choice? Internet Explorer is powerful like that. Well, the good news is that you've almost finished this book, and in just a few pages you will be in the appendixes. But before we part ways there is just one more example that needs to be done: let's (just for fun) take the FX demo application, the CORS version from earlier in this chapter, and merge in the *auth.html* example from earlier in this chapter. Therefore, the data flow won't start until you log in, which can be done with either basic auth or cookies. And let's (just for some *serious* fun[10]) make it work with all our target browsers, too. Well, as already explained, that means we simply cannot support IE8 and IE9: their CORS implementation is incompatible, by design, with wanting to authenticate. (The page will work and can be used with IE8; it will just break if you set the target URL to be a different origin.) However, *fx_client.auth.html* does do the check for Chromium 25 and earlier and Safari 6 and earlier, forcing them to use XHR instead of native SSE, so that CORS will work.

What that means is that only these browsers will use native SSE in this example: Firefox 10+, Opera 12+, Chrome 26+, Safari 7+. And, when using the "custom" login technique, all browsers will fallback to using the XHR technique when the origin is different (because XHR can do POST, while SSE only has cookies, and cookies cannot be sent to a different domain).

---

10. If you are cute, female, and actually thought that does sound like fun, we should get together…no, hang on, there has to be a catch. Nobody could be that perfect. You probably have some really weird hobby, involving toads or Excel or something.

Let's look at the backend first. The preceding sidebar explains why we have six files: *inc1* and *inc2* with most of the code (which is very similar to the code at the end of Chapter 7, so won't be shown again here), and then the other four files are similar to the files we saw with the three *auth_test.html* backends earlier in this chapter, the fourth variation being doing no authorization at all. The latter is useful to allow us to see what fails due to authorization issues, but it also represents what we would have if using the IP address as the authorization measure.

Both *fx_server.auth.noauth.php* and *fx_server.auth.apache.php* are the same code (because for *fx_server.auth.apache.php* Apache takes care of the authentication, and this script never gets called if the user is not valid):

```
<?php
include_once("fx_server.auth.inc1.php");
sendHeaders();
include_once("fx_server.auth.incs.php");
```

(The real code for *fx_server.auth.apache.php*, in addition to the this code, does a quick sanity check to make sure Apache authentication is working correctly.)

This is the version of the script *fx_server.auth.php.php* to handle doing the basic authentication inside our PHP script:

```php
<?php
include_once("fx_server.auth.inc1.php");

$user = @$_SERVER["PHP_AUTH_USER"];
$pw = @$_SERVER["PHP_AUTH_PW"];

$fromDB = '$2a$10$4LLeBta770Y0Z7795j.8'.
  'He/ZCQonnvImXIX0egalzE1MuWiEa6PQa';
if(!password_verify($pw, $fromDB)){
  header('WWW-Authenticate: Basic realm="SSE Book"');
  header("HTTP/1.0 401 Unauthorized");
  echo "Please authenticate.\n";
  exit;
  }

sendHeaders();

include_once("fx_server.auth.inc2.php");
```

Notice how the `sendHeaders()` call comes *after* the validation; if a problem occurs, we want to send back auth headers instead of SSE headers.

Finally, here is the most complex version, for doing a custom authentication based on cookie data. Except unlike the earlier example, it will accept the authentication data coming in by either cookies or POST data:

```php
<?php
include_once("fx_server.auth.inc1.php");

sendHeaders();

if(array_key_exists("login",$_COOKIE))$d = $_COOKIE["login"];
elseif(array_key_exists("login",$_POST))$d = $_POST["login"];
else{
  sendData(array(
    "action"=>"auth",
    "msg"=>"The login data is missing. Exiting."
    ));
  exit;
  }
if(strpos($d,",")===false){
  sendData(array(
    "action"=>"auth",
    "msg"=>"The login data is invalid. Exiting."
    ));
  exit;
  }
list($user,$pw) = explode(",",$d);
```

```
$fromDB = '$2a$10$4LLeBta770Y0Z7795j.8'.
  'He/ZCQonnvImXIX0egalzE1MuWiEa6PQa';
if(!password_verify($pw,$fromDB)){
  sendData(array(
    "action"=>"auth",
    "msg"=>"The login is bad. Exiting."
    ));
  exit;
  }

include_once("fx_server.auth.inc2.php");
```

sendHeaders() is called first, so that we can use sendData() to send back auth failures. They will be given to the browser as SSE messages.

 Troubleshooting an SSE backend from inside a browser can be a frustrating experience. But, unlike in earlier chapters, running PHP scripts directly from the command line is not a choice, because we need to specify headers and cookies. The best option for these quick tests is curl. Here are commands to test each of the three authentication approaches. (They assume the files are on *http://example.com*, in an *sse/* directory, so adapt them for your own installation.)

```
curl -uoreilly:test http://example.com/sse/fx_server.auth.apache.php
```

```
curl -uoreilly:test http://example.com/sse/fx_server.auth.php.php
```

```
curl --cookie "login=oreilly,test" ↵
    http://example.com/sse/fx_server.auth.custom.php
```

Add -v to see headers, or --trace - for information overload about what is passing back and forth. Add -H "Origin: http://127.0.0.1" to specify an origin.

Play around with the cookie or username:password values to see the error reporting.

Also make sure that these fail to connect:

```
curl http://example.com/sse/fx_server.auth.inc1.php
```

```
curl http://example.com/sse/fx_server.auth.inc2.php
```

Now to the frontend. When you load it, it looks like Figure 9-1.

Figure 9-1. Initial view of fx_client.auth.html

Following are the main differences from the previous versions, *fx_client.xhr.html* (end of Chapter 7) and *fx_client.cors.html* (earlier in this chapter):

- An HTML form to allow you to select: (1) the connection technique (SSE, XHR, iframe, long-poll) to use; (2) the target URL (e.g., you can change the domain name, or IP address, or switch between HTTP and HTTPS); and (3) the auth technique to use.

- A no-auth technique has been added.

- Older versions of Chrome and Safari are detected, based on their user-agents.

- When using the custom connection method *with a different origin*, XHR will POST the data, instead of using a cookie, and Native SSE will switch to also using POST by using the XHR fallback.

- Auth failures are intercepted and reported.

Taken together, that makes *fx_client.auth.html* the longest source code file, but a lot of the new code is form handling, which we will not look at in any depth here. I am also not going to look at the Chrome/Safari detection, which is just applying a few regexes.

The first code I will show is quite simple. When our custom authentication code (*fx_server.auth.custom.php*) has an error to report, it sends it back using the SSE data stream. It uses the action field set to `"auth"` to identify this. So, in `processOneLine()`, the following block has been added:

```
function processOneLine(s){
...
else if(d.action == "auth"){
  var x = document.getElementById("msg");
  x.innerHTML += "Auth Failure:" + d.msg + "<br/>";
  disconnect();
  }
}
```

The call to `disconnect()` is very important: we don't want it to keep trying to connect, and we don't even want a keep-alive mechanism to keep trying to connect.

Now that we have a form, what happens if the user clicks one of the connect buttons when a connection is already running? There is a new function called `reconnect()` that is used in this case:

```
this.reconnect = function(newUrl,newOptions){
disconnect();
url = newUrl;
for(var key in newOptions)
  options[key] = newOptions[key];
connect();
}
```

So, it first calls `disconnect()` to make sure not just that the current connection is closed, but that all timers get stopped. Then it sets the new URL, and any new options, and then it tries to connect to the new URL with those new settings.

The fallback from SSE to XHR has been implemented with the following highlighted changes to the `startSSE()` function:

```
function startEventSource(){
if(es){es.close();es=null;}
if(!isSameDomain()){
  if(options.post || isOldSafariChrome){startXHR();return;}
  }
if(options.post)document.cookie = options.post +"; path=/";
var u = url;
if(lastId)u += "lastId="
  + encodeURIComponent(lastId) + "&";
es = new EventSource(u, { withCredentials: true } );
es.addEventListener("message", function(e){processOneLine(e.data);},false);
es.addEventListener("error", handleError, false);
}
```

As background to this, the `options` object now has an optional `post` element, in which we put `"login=username,password"` when using custom authentication. The first of the highlighted clauses is saying that when connecting to a different origin and wanting to send a cookie it will not work, so use the XHR approach instead. The second part says if wanting to send a cookie and connecting to the same origin, then set a cookie.

The `|| isOldSafariChrome` part is because old browsers that haven't implemented CORS for SSE will not work with a different origin, whether sending a cookie or not, so they should use XHR here instead.

The second half of that is how to handle POST in `startXHR()`:

```
function startXHR(){
...
var ds = null;
fallback = "xhr=1&t=" + (new Date().getTime());
if(options.post){
  xhr.open("POST", url, true);
  xhr.setRequestHeader("Content-type", "application/x-www-form-urlencoded");
```

```
    ds = fallback + "&" + options.post;
    }
else{
  xhr.open("GET", url + fallback, true);
    }
...
xhr.send(ds);
}
```

 The code you will see in *fx_client.xhr.html* is quite different from this, because it has been refactored to move most of the code into a helper function, called `useXMLHttpRequest()`, that is then shared between both `startXHR()` and `startLongPoll()`.

So, when `options.post` is not set, it is the same as the previous code: `xhr` and `t` will be sent in the URL. But when `options.post` is set, we have to set an extra header, then build all the data we want to send in `ds`, which is then passed to `xhr.send(ds)`.

And that is it. Try a few tests. For example, if you are browsing it at *http://example.com/sse/listings/fx_client.auth.html*, then change "Base URL to connect to" to "https://example.com/sse/listings/", or "http://www1.example.com/sse/listings/", etc. Then try each of the buttons, and watch to see if the data comes through, or if you get an authentication error. And, assuming data comes through, have a look in Firebug (or whatever developer tools you are using) to see if the connection is using SSE or XHR or long-poll, and if it is using GET or POST, and to see what cookies are being sent.

The Future Holds More of the Same

This has been a long and complicated chapter. It would have been considerably simpler if (1) the SSE standard, and its implementations, allowed us to set our own headers and send POST data, as we can with Ajax; (2) old browsers did not exist.

Based on the experience of the past 15 years, old browsers and browser bugs will always be with us, and we just have to be prepared to cope with them. However, for dealing with point (1) (the limitations of the SSE standard), the fact that we had already written the fallbacks for the older browsers meant that we could relatively easily handle those limitations. In fact, the workaround ended up as simple as this:

```
if(!isSameDomain()){
  if(options.post || isOldSafariChrome){startXHR();return;}
  }
```

The Server-Sent Events API is still quite new, and I would not be surprised if it gets some improvements in the next year or two. But it is also very useful even in its current form, and I hope you find many good uses for it in your own projects.

The SSE Standard

The official standard for Server-Sent Events is a "W3C Candidate Recommendation" at the time of writing. The latest published version is available from *http:// www.w3.org/TR/eventsource/*.

W3C Candidate Recommendation 11 December 2012

This Version:
> *http://www.w3.org/TR/2012/CR-eventsource-20121211/*

Latest Published Version:
> *http://www.w3.org/TR/eventsource/*

Latest Editor's Draft:
> *http://dev.w3.org/html5/eventsource/*

Previous Versions:
> *http://www.w3.org/TR/2012/WD-eventsource-20121023/*

> *http://www.w3.org/TR/2012/WD-eventsource-20120426/*

> *http://www.w3.org/TR/2011/WD-eventsource-20111020/*

> *http://www.w3.org/TR/2011/WD-eventsource-20110310/*

> *http://www.w3.org/TR/2011/WD-eventsource-20110208/*

> *http://www.w3.org/TR/2009/WD-eventsource-20091222/*

> *http://www.w3.org/TR/2009/WD-eventsource-20091029/*

> *http://www.w3.org/TR/2009/WD-eventsource-20090423/*

Editor:
> Ian Hickson (*ian@hixie.ch*), Google, Inc.

The bulk of the text of this specification is also available in the WHATWG Web Applications 1.0 specification, under a license that permits reuse of the specification text.

Abstract

This specification defines an API for opening an HTTP connection for receiving push notifications from a server in the form of DOM events. The API is designed such that it can be extended to work with other push notification schemes such as Push SMS.

Status of This Document

This section describes the status of this document at the time of its publication. Other documents may supersede this document. A list of current W3C publications and the latest revision of this technical report can be found in the W3C technical reports index at http://www.w3.org/TR/.

If you wish to make comments regarding this document in a manner that is tracked by the W3C, please submit them via using our public bug database. If you do not have an account then you can enter feedback using the form at *http://www.w3.org/TR/eventsource/*.

You can also e-mail feedback to *public-webapps@w3.org* (subscribe, archives), or *whatwg@whatwg.org* (subscribe, archives). All feedback is welcome.

Notifications of changes to this specification are sent along with notifications of changes to related specifications using the following mechanisms:

E-mail notifications of changes
    Commit-Watchers mailing list (complete source diffs): *http://lists.whatwg.org/listinfo.cgi/commit-watchers-whatwg.org*

Browsable version-control record of all changes:
    CVSWeb interface with side-by-side diffs: *http://dev.w3.org/cvsweb/html5/*

    Annotated summary with unified diffs: *http://html5.org/tools/web-apps-tracker*

    Raw Subversion interface: `svn checkout http://svn.whatwg.org/webapps/`

The W3C Web Applications Working Group is the W3C working group responsible for this specification's progress along the W3C Recommendation track. This specification is the 11 December 2012 Candidate Recommendation. There were no comments or bugs submitted against the 23 October 2012 Last Call Working Draft.

Publication as a Candidate Recommendation does not imply endorsement by the W3C Membership. This is a draft document and may be updated, replaced or obsoleted by other documents at any time. It is inappropriate to cite this document as other than work in progress.

This document was produced by a group operating under the 5 February 2004 W3C Patent Policy. W3C maintains a public list of any patent disclosures made in connection with the deliverables of the group; that page also includes instructions for disclosing a patent. An individual who has actual knowledge of a patent which the individual believes contains Essential Claim(s) must disclose the information in accordance with section 6 of the W3C Patent Policy.

Candidate Recommendation Exit Criteria

To exit the Candidate Recommendation (CR) stage, the following criteria must have been met:

1. There will be at least two interoperable implementations passing all approved test cases in the test suite for this specification. An implementation is to be available (i.e. for download), shipping (i.e. not private), and not experimental (i.e. intended for a wide audience). The working group will decide when the test suite is of sufficient quality to test interoperability and will produce an implementation report (hosted together with the test suite).

2. A minimum of two months of the CR stage will have elapsed (i.e. not until after 11 February 2013). This is to ensure that enough time is given for any remaining major errors to be caught. The CR period will be extended if implementations are slow to appear.

Table of Contents

1 Introduction

This section is non-normative.

To enable servers to push data to Web pages over HTTP or using dedicated server-push protocols, this specification introduces the EventSource interface.

Using this API consists of creating an EventSource object and registering an event listener.

```
var source = new
    EventSource('updates.cgi'); source.onmessage = function (event) {
    alert(event.data); };
```

On the server-side, the script ("updates.cgi" in this case) sends messages in the following form, with the text/event-stream MIME type:

```
data: This is the first message.
    data: This is the second message, it data: has two lines. data: This is
    the third message.
```

Authors can separate events by using different event types. Here is a stream that has two event types, "add" and "remove":

```
event: add data: 73857293 event:
    remove data: 2153 event: add data: 113411
```

The script to handle such a stream would look like this (where addHandler and removeHandler are functions that take one argument, the event):

```
var source = new
    EventSource('updates.cgi'); source.addEventListener('add', addHandler,
    false); source.addEventListener('remove', removeHandler, false);
```

The default event type is "message".

Event stream requests can be redirected using HTTP 301 and 307 redirects as with normal HTTP requests. Clients will reconnect if the connection is closed; a client can be told to stop reconnecting using the HTTP 204 No Content response code.

Using this API rather than emulating it using XMLHttpRequest or an iframe allows the user agent to make better use of network resources in cases where the user agent implementor and the network operator are able to coordinate in advance. Amongst other benefits, this can result in significant savings in battery life on portable devices. This is discussed further in the section below on connectionless push.

---

2 Conformance requirements

All diagrams, examples, and notes in this specification are non-normative, as are all sections explicitly marked non-normative. Everything else in this specification is normative.

The key words "MUST", "MUST NOT", "REQUIRED", "SHOULD", "SHOULD NOT", "RECOMMENDED", "MAY", and "OPTIONAL" in the normative parts of this document are to be interpreted as described in RFC2119. For readability, these words do not appear in all uppercase letters in this specification. [RFC2119]

Requirements phrased in the imperative as part of algorithms (such as "strip any leading space characters" or "return false and abort these steps") are to be interpreted with the meaning of the key word ("must", "should", "may", etc) used in introducing the algorithm.

Some conformance requirements are phrased as requirements on attributes, methods or objects. Such requirements are to be interpreted as requirements on user agents.

Conformance requirements phrased as algorithms or specific steps may be implemented in any manner, so long as the end result is equivalent. (In particular, the algorithms defined in this specification are intended to be easy to follow, and not intended to be performant.)

The only conformance class defined by this specification is user agents.

User agents may impose implementation-specific limits on otherwise unconstrained inputs, e.g. to prevent denial of service attacks, to guard against running out of memory, or to work around platform-specific limitations.

When support for a feature is disabled (e.g. as an emergency measure to mitigate a security problem, or to aid in development, or for performance reasons), user agents must act as if they had no support for the feature whatsoever, and as if the feature was not mentioned in this specification. For example, if a particular feature is accessed via an attribute in a Web IDL interface, the attribute itself would be omitted from the objects that implement that interface — leaving the attribute on the object but making it return null or throw an exception is insufficient.

2.1 Dependencies

This specification relies on several other underlying specifications.

HTML
Many fundamental concepts from HTML are used by this specification. [HTML]

WebIDL
The IDL blocks in this specification use the semantics of the WebIDL specification. [WEBIDL]

WebMessaging
MessageEvent is defined in [WEBMESSAGING].

3 Terminology

The construction "a Foo object", where Foo is actually an interface, is sometimes used instead of the more accurate "an object implementing the interface Foo."

The term DOM is used to refer to the API set made available to scripts in Web applications, and does not necessarily imply the existence of an actual Document object or of any other Node objects as defined in the DOM Core specifications. [DOMCORE]

An IDL attribute is said to be *getting* when its value is being retrieved (e.g. by author script), and is said to be *setting* when a new value is assigned to it.

4 The EventSource interface

```
[Constructor(DOMString url,
    optional EventSourceInit eventSourceInitDict)] interface EventSource :
    EventTarget { readonly attribute DOMString url; readonly attribute
    boolean withCredentials; // ready state const unsigned short CONNECTING
    = 0; const unsigned short OPEN = 1; const unsigned short CLOSED = 2;
    readonly attribute unsigned short readyState; // networking attribute
    EventHandler onopen; attribute EventHandler onmessage; attribute
    EventHandler onerror; void close(); }; dictionary EventSourceInit {
    boolean withCredentials = false; };
```

The EventSource() constructor takes one or two arguments. The first specifies the URL to which to connect. The second specifies the settings, if any, in the form of an EventSourceInit dictionary. When the EventSource() constructor is invoked, the UA must run these steps:

1. Resolve the URL specified in the first argument, relative to the entry script's base URL. [HTML]

2. If the previous step failed, then throw a SyntaxError exception.

3. Create a new EventSource object.

4. Let CORS mode be Anonymous.

5. If the second argument is present, and the withCredentials dictionary member has the value true, then set CORS mode to Use Credentials and initialize the new EventSource object's withCredentials attribute to true.

6. Return the new EventSource object, and continue these steps in the background (without blocking scripts).

7. Do a potentially CORS-enabled fetch of the resulting absolute URL using the entry script's referrer source, with the *mode* being CORS mode, and the *origin* being the

entry script's origin, and process the resource obtained in this fashion, if any, as described below.

 The definition of the fetching algorithm (which is used by CORS) is such that if the browser is already fetching the resource identified by the given absolute URL, that connection can be reused, instead of a new connection being established. All messages received up to this point are dispatched immediately, in this case.

This constructor must be visible when the script's global object is either a Window object or an object implementing the WorkerUtils interface.

The url attribute must return the absolute URL that resulted from resolving the value that was passed to the constructor.

The withCredentials attribute must return the value to which it was last initialized. When the object is created, it must be initialized to false.

The readyState attribute represents the state of the connection. It can have the following values:

CONNECTING *(numeric value 0)*
> The connection has not yet been established, or it was closed and the user agent is reconnecting.

OPEN *(numeric value 1)*
> The user agent has an open connection and is dispatching events as it receives them.

CLOSED *(numeric value 2)*
> The connection is not open, and the user agent is not trying to reconnect. Either there was a fatal error or the close() method was invoked.

When the object is created its readyState must be set to CONNECTING (0). The rules given below for handling the connection define when the value changes.

The close() method must abort any instances of the fetch algorithm started for this EventSource object, and must set the readyState attribute to CLOSED.

The following are the event handlers (and their corresponding event handler event types) that must be supported, as IDL attributes, by all objects implementing the EventSource interface:

Event handler	Event handler event type
onopen	open
onmessage	message
onerror	error

In addition to the above, each EventSource object has the following associated with it:

- A reconnection time, in milliseconds. This must initially be a user-agent-defined value, probably in the region of a few seconds.
- A last event ID string. This must initially be the empty string.

These values are not currently exposed on the interface.

5 Processing model

The resource indicated in the argument to the EventSource constructor is fetched when the constructor is run.

For HTTP connections, the Accept header may be included; if included, it must contain only formats of event framing that are supported by the user agent (one of which must be text/event-stream, as described below).

If the event source's last event ID string is not the empty string, then a Last-Event-ID HTTP header must be included with the request, whose value is the value of the event source's last event ID string, encoded as UTF-8.

User agents should use the Cache-Control: no-cache header in requests to bypass any caches for requests of event sources. (This header is not a custom request header, so the user agent will still use the CORS simple cross-origin request mechanism.) User agents should ignore HTTP cache headers in the response, never caching event sources.

As data is received, the tasks queued by the networking task source to handle the data must act as follows.

HTTP 200 OK responses with a Content-Type header specifying the type text/event-stream, ignoring any MIME type parameters, must be processed line by line as described below.

When a successful response with a supported MIME type is received, such that the user agent begins parsing the contents of the stream, the user agent must announce the connection.

The task that the networking task source places on the task queue once the fetching algorithm for such a resource (with the correct MIME type) has completed must cause the user agent to asynchronously reestablish the connection. This applies whether the connection is closed gracefully or unexpectedly. It doesn't apply for the error conditions listed below except where explicitly specified.

HTTP 200 OK responses that have a Content-Type specifying an unsupported type, or that have no Content-Type at all, must cause the user agent to fail the connection.

HTTP 305 Use Proxy, 401 Unauthorized, and 407 Proxy Authentication Required should be treated transparently as for any other subresource.

HTTP 301 Moved Permanently, 302 Found, 303 See Other, and 307 Temporary Redirect responses are handled by the fetching and CORS algorithms. In the case of 301 redirects, the user agent must also remember the new URL so that subsequent requests for this resource for this `EventSource` object start with the URL given for the last 301 seen for requests for this object.

HTTP 500 Internal Server Error, 502 Bad Gateway, 503 Service Unavailable, and 504 Gateway Timeout responses, and any network error that prevents the connection from being established in the first place (e.g. DNS errors), must cause the user agent to asynchronously reestablish the connection.

Any other HTTP response code not listed here must cause the user agent to fail the connection.

For non-HTTP protocols, UAs should act in equivalent ways.

When a user agent is to announce the connection, the user agent must queue a task which, if the `readyState` attribute is set to a value other than `CLOSED`, sets the `ready State` attribute to `OPEN` and fires a simple event named open at the `EventSource` object.

When a user agent is to reestablish the connection, the user agent must run the following steps. These steps are run asynchronously, not as part of a task. (The tasks that it queues, of course, are run like normal tasks and not asynchronously.)

1. Queue a task to run the following steps:

   a. If the `readyState` attribute is set to `CLOSED`, abort the task.

   b. Set the `readyState` attribute to `CONNECTING`.

   c. Fire a simple event named `error` at the `EventSource` object.

2. Wait a delay equal to the reconnection time of the event source.

3. Optionally, wait some more. In particular, if the previous attempt failed, then user agents might introduce an exponential backoff delay to avoid overloading a potentially already overloaded server. Alternatively, if the operating system has reported that there is no network connectivity, user agents might wait for the operating system to announce that the network connection has returned before retrying.

4. Wait until the aforementioned task has run, if it has not yet run.

5. Queue a task to run the following steps:

   a. If the `readyState` attribute is not set to `CONNECTING`, abort these steps.

   b. Perform a potentially CORS-enabled fetch of the absolute URL of the event source resource, using the same *referrer source*, and with the same *mode* and *origin*, as those used in the original request triggered by the `EventSource()`

constructor, and process the resource obtained in this fashion, if any, as described earlier in this section.

When a user agent is to fail the connection, the user agent must queue a task which, if the `readyState` attribute is set to a value other than `CLOSED`, sets the `readyState` attribute to `CLOSED` and fires a simple event named `error` at the `EventSource` object. **Once the user agent has failed the connection, it does *not* attempt to reconnect!**

The task source for any tasks that are queued by `EventSource` objects is the remote event task source.

6 Parsing an event stream

This event stream format's MIME type is `text/event-stream`.

The event stream format is as described by the `stream` production of the following ABNF, the character set for which is Unicode. [ABNF]

```
stream = [ bom ] *event event =
*( comment / field ) end-of-line comment = colon *any-char end-of-line
field = 1*name-char [ colon [ space ] *any-char ] end-of-line
end-of-line = ( cr lf / cr / lf ) ; characters lf = %x000A ; U+000A LINE
FEED (LF) cr = %x000D ; U+000D CARRIAGE RETURN (CR) space = %x0020 ;
U+0020 SPACE colon = %x003A ; U+003A COLON (:) bom = %xFEFF ; U+FEFF
BYTE ORDER MARK name-char = %x0000-0009 / %x000B-000C / %x000E-0039 /
%x003B-10FFFF ; a Unicode character other than U+000A LINE FEED (LF), ;
U+000D CARRIAGE RETURN (CR), or U+003A COLON (:) any-char = %x0000-0009
/ %x000B-000C / %x000E-10FFFF ; a Unicode character other than U+000A
LINE FEED (LF) ; or U+000D CARRIAGE RETURN (CR)
```

Event streams in this format must always be encoded as UTF-8. [RFC3629]

Lines must be separated by either a U+000D CARRIAGE RETURN U+000A LINE FEED (CRLF) character pair, a single U+000A LINE FEED (LF) character, or a single U+000D CARRIAGE RETURN (CR) character.

Since connections established to remote servers for such resources are expected to be long-lived, UAs should ensure that appropriate buffering is used. In particular, while line buffering with lines are defined to end with a single U+000A LINE FEED (LF) character is safe, block buffering or line buffering with different expected line endings can cause delays in event dispatch.

7 Interpreting an event stream

Streams must be decoded as UTF-8, with error handling. [HTML]

One leading U+FEFF BYTE ORDER MARK character must be ignored if any are present.

The stream must then be parsed by reading everything line by line, with a U+000D CARRIAGE RETURN U+000A LINE FEED (CRLF) character pair, a single U+000A LINE FEED (LF) character not preceded by a U+000D CARRIAGE RETURN (CR) character, and a single U+000D CARRIAGE RETURN (CR) character not followed by a U+000A LINE FEED (LF) character being the ways in which a line can end.

When a stream is parsed, a data buffer, an event type buffer, and a last event ID buffer must be associated with it. They must be initialized to the empty string

Lines must be processed, in the order they are received, as follows:

If the line is empty (a blank line)
> Dispatch the event, as defined below.

If the line starts with a U+003A COLON character (:)
> Ignore the line.

If the line contains a U+003A COLON character (:)
> Collect the characters on the line before the first U+003A COLON character (:), and let field be that string.
>
> Collect the characters on the line after the first U+003A COLON character (:), and let value be that string. If value starts with a U+0020 SPACE character, remove it from value.
>
> Process the field using the steps described below, using field as the field name and value as the field value.

Otherwise, the string is not empty but does not contain a U+003A COLON character (:)
> Process the field using the steps described below, using the whole line as the field name, and the empty string as the field value.

Once the end of the file is reached, any pending data must be discarded. (If the file ends in the middle of an event, before the final empty line, the incomplete event is not dispatched.)

The steps to process the field given a field name and a field value depend on the field name, as given in the following list. Field names must be compared literally, with no case folding performed.

If the field name is "event"
> Set the event type buffer to field value.

If the field name is "data"
> Append the field value to the data buffer, then append a single U+000A LINE FEED (LF) character to the data buffer.

If the field name is "id"
> Set the last event ID buffer to the field value.

If the field name is "retry"
> If the field value consists of only ASCII digits, then interpret the field value as an integer in base ten, and set the event stream's reconnection time to that integer. Otherwise, ignore the field.

Otherwise
> The field is ignored.

When the user agent is required to dispatch the event, then the user agent must act as follows:

1. Set the last event ID string of the event source to value of the last event ID buffer. The buffer does not get reset, so the last event ID string of the event source remains set to this value until the next time it is set by the server.

2. If the data buffer is an empty string, set the data buffer and the event type buffer to the empty string and abort these steps.

3. If the data buffer's last character is a U+000A LINE FEED (LF) character, then remove the last character from the data buffer.

4. Create an event that uses the `MessageEvent` interface, with the event type `message`, which does not bubble, is not cancelable, and has no default action. The `data` attribute must be initialized to the value of the data buffer, the `origin` attribute must be initialized to the Unicode serialization of the origin of the event stream's final URL (i.e. the URL after redirects), and the `lastEventId` attribute must be initialized to the last event ID string of the event source. This event is not trusted.

5. If the event type buffer has a value other than the empty string, change the type of the newly created event to equal the value of the event type buffer.

6. Set the data buffer and the event type buffer to the empty string.

7. Queue a task which, if the `readyState` attribute is set to a value other than `CLOSED`, dispatches the newly created event at the `EventSource` object.

 If an event doesn't have an "id" field, but an earlier event did set the event source's last event ID string, then the event's `lastEventId` field will be set to the value of whatever the last seen "id" field was.

The following event stream, once followed by a blank line:

```
data: YHOO data: +2 data: 10
```

…would cause an event message with the interface MessageEvent to be dispatched on the EventSource object. The event's data attribute would contain the string YHOO\n +2\n10 (where \n represents a newline).

This could be used as follows:

```
var stocks = new
    EventSource("http://stocks.example.com/ticker.php"); stocks.onmessage =
    function (event) { var data = event.data.split('\n');
    updateStocks(data[0], data[1], data[2]); };
```

…where updateStocks() is a function defined as:

```
function updateStocks(symbol,
    delta, value) { ... }
```

…or some such.

The following stream contains four blocks. The first block has just a comment, and will fire nothing. The second block has two fields with names "data" and "id" respectively; an event will be fired for this block, with the data "first event", and will then set the last event ID to "1" so that if the connection died between this block and the next, the server would be sent a Last-Event-ID header with the value "1". The third block fires an event with data "second event", and also has an "id" field, this time with no value, which resets the last event ID to the empty string (meaning no Last-Event-ID header will now be sent in the event of a reconnection being attempted). Finally, the last block just fires an event with the data " third event" (with a single leading space character). Note that the last still has to end with a blank line, the end of the stream is not enough to trigger the dispatch of the last event.

```
: test stream data: first event
    id: 1 data:second event id data: third event
```

The following stream fires two events:

```
data data data data:
```

The first block fires events with the data set to the empty string, as would the last block if it was followed by a blank line. The middle block fires an event with the data set to a single newline character. The last block is discarded because it is not followed by a blank line.

The following stream fires two identical events:

```
data:test data: test
```

This is because the space after the colon is ignored if present.

8 Notes

Legacy proxy servers are known to, in certain cases, drop HTTP connections after a short timeout. To protect against such proxy servers, authors can include a comment line (one starting with a ':' character) every 15 seconds or so.

Authors wishing to relate event source connections to each other or to specific documents previously served might find that relying on IP addresses doesn't work, as individual clients can have multiple IP addresses (due to having multiple proxy servers) and individual IP addresses can have multiple clients (due to sharing a proxy server). It is better to include a unique identifier in the document when it is served and then pass that identifier as part of the URL when the connection is established.

Authors are also cautioned that HTTP chunking can have unexpected negative effects on the reliability of this protocol. Where possible, chunking should be disabled for serving event streams unless the rate of messages is high enough for this not to matter.

Clients that support HTTP's per-server connection limitation might run into trouble when opening multiple pages from a site if each page has an `EventSource` to the same domain. Authors can avoid this using the relatively complex mechanism of using unique domain names per connection, or by allowing the user to enable or disable the `EventSource` functionality on a per-page basis, or by sharing a single `EventSource` object using a shared worker. [WEBWORKERS]

9 Connectionless push and other features

User agents running in controlled environments, e.g. browsers on mobile handsets tied to specific carriers, may offload the management of the connection to a proxy on the network. In such a situation, the user agent for the purposes of conformance is considered to include both the handset software and the network proxy.

For example, a browser on a mobile device, after having established a connection, might detect that it is on a supporting network and request that a proxy server on the network take over the management of the connection. The timeline for such a situation might be as follows:

1. Browser connects to a remote HTTP server and requests the resource specified by the author in the `EventSource` constructor.

2. The server sends occasional messages.

3. In between two messages, the browser detects that it is idle except for the network activity involved in keeping the TCP connection alive, and decides to switch to sleep mode to save power.

4. The browser disconnects from the server.

5. The browser contacts a service on the network, and requests that that service, a "push proxy", maintain the connection instead.

6. The "push proxy" service contacts the remote HTTP server and requests the resource specified by the author in the EventSource constructor (possibly including a Last-Event-ID HTTP header, etc).

7. The browser allows the mobile device to go to sleep.

8. The server sends another message.

9. The "push proxy" service uses a technology such as OMA push to convey the event to the mobile device, which wakes only enough to process the event and then returns to sleep.

This can reduce the total data usage, and can therefore result in considerable power savings.

As well as implementing the existing API and text/event-stream wire format as defined by this specification and in more distributed ways as described above, formats of event framing defined by other applicable specifications may be supported. This specification does not define how they are to be parsed or processed.

10 Garbage collection

While an EventSource object's readyState is CONNECTING, and the object has one or more event listeners registered for open, message or error events, there must be a strong reference from the Window or WorkerUtils object that the EventSource object's constructor was invoked from to the EventSource object itself.

While an EventSource object's readyState is OPEN, and the object has one or more event listeners registered for message or error events, there must be a strong reference from the Window or WorkerUtils object that the EventSource object's constructor was invoked from to the EventSource object itself.

While there is a task queued by an EventSource object on the remote event task source, there must be a strong reference from the Window or WorkerUtils object that the EventSource object's constructor was invoked from to that EventSource object.

If a user agent is to forcibly close an EventSource object (this happens when a Document object goes away permanently), the user agent must abort any instances of the fetch algorithm started for this EventSource object, and must set the readyState attribute to CLOSED.

If an EventSource object is garbage collected while its connection is still open, the user agent must abort any instance of the fetch algorithm opened by this EventSource.

It's possible for one active network connection to be shared by multiple EventSource objects and their fetch algorithms, which is why the above is phrased in terms of aborting the fetch algorithm and not the actual underlying download.

11 IANA considerations

11.1 `text/event-stream`

This registration is for community review and will be submitted to the IESG for review, approval, and registration with IANA.

Type name:
  text

Subtype name:
  event-stream

Required parameters:
  No parameters

Optional parameters:
  `charset`

> The `charset` parameter may be provided. The parameter's value must be "`utf-8`". This parameter serves no purpose; it is only allowed for compatibility with legacy servers.

Encoding considerations:
  8bit (always UTF-8)

Security considerations:

> An event stream from an origin distinct from the origin of the content consuming the event stream can result in information leakage. To avoid this, user agents are required to apply CORS semantics. [CORS]

> Event streams can overwhelm a user agent; a user agent is expected to apply suitable restrictions to avoid depleting local resources because of an overabundance of information from an event stream.

> Servers can be overwhelmed if a situation develops in which the server is causing clients to reconnect rapidly. Servers should use a 5xx status code to indicate capacity problems, as this will prevent conforming clients from reconnecting automatically.

Interoperability considerations:

> Rules for processing both conforming and non-conforming content are defined in this specification.

Published specification:
This document is the relevant specification.

Applications that use this media type:
Web browsers and tools using Web services.

Additional information:
Magic number(s):
No sequence of bytes can uniquely identify an event stream.

File extension(s):
No specific file extensions are recommended for this type.

Macintosh file type code(s):
No specific Macintosh file type codes are recommended for this type.

Person & email address to contact for further information:
Ian Hickson (*ian@hixie.ch*)

Intended usage:
Common

Restrictions on usage:
This format is only expected to be used by dynamic open-ended streams served using HTTP or a similar protocol. Finite resources are not expected to be labeled with this type.

Author:
Ian Hickson <ian@hixie.ch>

Change controller:
W3C

Fragment identifiers have no meaning with `text/event-stream` resources.

11.2 `Last-Event-ID`

This section describes a header field for registration in the Permanent Message Header Field Registry. [RFC3864]

Header field name:
Last-Event-ID

Applicable protocol:
http

Status:
standard

Author/Change controller:
    W3C

Specification document(s):
    This document is the relevant specification.

Related information:
    None.

References

All references are normative unless marked "Non-normative".

[ABNF]
    Augmented BNF for Syntax Specifications: ABNF, D. Crocker, P. Overell. IETF.

[CORS]
    Cross-Origin Resource Sharing, A. van Kesteren. W3C.

[DOMCORE]
    DOM4, A. van Kesteren. W3C.

[HTML]
    HTML5, I. Hickson. W3C.

[RFC2119]
    Key words for use in RFCs to Indicate Requirement Levels, S. Bradner. IETF.

[RFC3629]
    UTF-8, a transformation format of ISO 10646, F. Yergeau. IETF.

[RFC3864]
    Registration Procedures for Message Header Fields, G. Klyne, M. Nottingham, J. Mogul. IETF.

[WEBIDL]
    Web IDL, C. McCormack. W3C.

[WEBWORKERS]
    Web Workers, I. Hickson. W3C.

[WEBMESSAGING]
    Web Messaging, I. Hickson. W3C.

Acknowledgements

For a full list of acknowledgements, please see the HTML specification. [HTML]

Refactor: JavaScript Globals, Objects, and Closures

You know globals are wrong, don't you? The prim and proper computer science types tell us that. But they just make life so much easier! No messing about passing long parameter lists (or refactoring long parameter lists into a single object parameter, which then doubles the length of the body code to use). No worrying about scope: they are just there (well, in JavaScript and many languages they are; in PHP you have to either use the `globals` keyword to declare which globals to use, or use the `$_GLOBALS[]` superglobal). When you need to modify them, no worrying about having to return values or reference parameters. So what were the good reasons for not using globals? Testing. Yawn. Encapsulation. Side effects. Blah, blah, blah.

But, in the context of data push applications, there is one situation where globals are going to trip us up: when you need to make two or more connections.

 This appendix just talks about refactoring the JavaScript to not use globals. It is an appendix because it shows general-purpose Java-Script techniques: there is nothing specifically about data push here (except the example code, of course). Basically, it is an appendix because it got a bit too big for a sidebar in the main text!

Introducing the Example

I will use a stripped-down SSE example. This code won't have interesting data, and it won't have the fallback code for the older browsers. None of that affects the decision of which approach is better, it just adds more lines of code.

First, the backend:

```php
<?php
header("Content-Type: text/event-stream");

function sendData($data){
echo "data:";
echo json_encode($data)."\n";
echo "\n";  //Extra blank line
@flush();@ob_flush();
}

//-------------------------------------
while(true){
  switch(rand(1,10)){
    case 1:
      sendData( array("comeBackIn10s" => true) );
      exit;
    case 2:
      sendData( array("msg" => "About to sleep 10s") );
      sleep(10);  //Force a keep-alive timeout
      break;
    default:
      sendData( array("t" => date("Y-m-d H:i:s")) );
      sleep(1);
      break;
  }
}
```

The `while(true)switch(rand(1,10)){...}` idiom means loop forever and choose what to do on each loop randomly. Eighty percent of the time it will end up in the `default:` clause, and just send back a datestamp. You've seen code like this back in the very first examples in Chapter 2, so I won't explain it or the `sendData()` function again.

Of more interest is that 10 percent of the time (`case 2:`) it will go to sleep for 10 seconds. This is to simulate a dead connection: 10 seconds is enough because I will be setting the keep-alive timeout in the JavaScript to just 5 seconds. I also send back a message so we can see when this happens.

And what about `case 1:`? This sends back a special flag, and then dies. This represents the scheduled shutdown idea that we look at in "Adding Scheduled Shutdowns/Reconnects" on page 68. As the name of the flag suggests, we want the client to leave us alone for 10 seconds, then reconnect.

How does the frontend look? Like this:

```html
<!doctype html>
<html>
  <head>
    <meta charset="UTF-8">
    <title>SSE: Basic With Sleep: Globals</title>
```

```
    </head>
    <body>
      <pre id="x">Initializing...</pre>
      <script>
      var url = "basic_with_sleep.php";
      var es = null;
      var keepaliveSecs = 5;
      var keepaliveTimer = null;

      function gotActivity(){
      if(keepaliveTimer != null)
        clearTimeout(keepaliveTimer);
      keepaliveTimer = setTimeout(
        connect, keepaliveSecs * 1000);
      }

      function connect(){
      document.getElementById("x").
        innerHTML += "\nIn connect";
      if(es)es.close();
      gotActivity();
      es = new EventSource(url);
      es.addEventListener("message",
        function(e){processOneLine(e.data);},
        false);
      }

      function processOneLine(s){
      gotActivity();
      document.getElementById("x").
        innerHTML += "\n" + s;
      var d = JSON.parse(s);

      if(d.comeBackIn10s){
        if(keepaliveTimer != null)
          clearTimeout(keepaliveTimer);
        if(es)es.close();
        setTimeout(connect,10*1000);
        }

      }

      setTimeout(connect,100);

      </script>
  </body>
  </html>
```

If you have read Chapter 5, you will recognize that the keepaliveSecs and keepalive
Timer globals and the gotActivity() function are working together to make sure the
connection is always up. The connect() function does the job of both connect() and
startEventSource() in most of the code examples in this book; this is just a simplifi-

cation because there is no fallback handling. `processOneLine()` just outputs the raw JSON it is receiving. The second half of `processOneLine()` is where the `comeBack In10s` message is handled (this is the inline equivalent of the `temporarilyDiscon nect()` function introduced in Chapter 5).

If you are reading this before reading Chapters 3, 4, and 5, and it is causing your brow to crinkle, just relax about exactly what the code is doing. The important things that I want to point out here are:

- There are four globals (one is a parameter, the other three are worker variables).
- Each of the four functions uses at least a couple of those globals.
- `connect()` is being called from three different places:
  — The initial global code call (actually after 100ms)
  — After a keep-alive timeout
  — After a request to come back in 10 seconds
- When `connect()` is called, it closes the old connection before starting a new one. This is the sole reason that `es` (the `EventSource` object) is captured into a global.

Load *basic_with_sleep.html* into your browser and try it out. It will look something like this:

```
Initializing...
In connect
{"t":"2014-02-28 09:46:34"}
{"t":"2014-02-28 09:46:35"}
{"t":"2014-02-28 09:46:36"}
{"msg":"About to sleep 10s"}
In connect
{"t":"2014-02-28 09:46:42"}
{"comeBackIn10s":true}
In connect
{"t":"2014-02-28 09:46:53"}
{"t":"2014-02-28 09:46:54"}
.
.
.
```

When it goes to sleep we get no fresh data, so after 5 seconds the keep-alive timer kicks in, closes the old connection, and starts a new one. So you see a 6-second gap. When it says come back in 10 seconds, we shut down the connection, switch off the keep-alive timer, and politely obey with a 10-second nap, so there is an 11-second gap in the time-stamps.

The Problem Is...

...two connections. Find *basic_with_sleep.two.html* in the book's source code and try it out. I'm not showing the code here because it is too gruesome. I now have seven globals, and eight global functions. Making this code required a lot of concentration and still I got it wrong, and had to debug my typos in Firebug. OK, game, set, and match to the computer scientists. You were right. Globals are Bad.

 To be fair, the code in *basic_with_sleep.two.html* was a really crude, naive approach. A couple of helper functions that take parameters could made it look not so bad. (Like a wig and a Jenna-Louise Coleman mask on Frankenstein. But as you lean in for the kiss you realize something does not smell quite right...)

So, something has to be done. I am going to look at a couple of solutions that JavaScript offers, and compare them.

JavaScript Objects and Constructors

JavaScript is an object-oriented language. Or maybe it isn't and just pretends to be. If you think arguing points like this is a Fun Thing To Do, do it on your own time, not now, not here. The example code looks a bit like an object, so how about making it into a JavaScript object? The four globals could be the member variables. The four functions would be the member functions.

One great resource on this subject is *Secrets of the JavaScript Ninja* by John Resig and Bear Bibeault (Manning, 2012).

Let's have a quick recap on JavaScript objects. But before that, a quick recap on JavaScript functions, and especially the this variable. Functions in JavaScript are first-class objects, which means they can be passed around, it is easy to define callbacks, and they can even have properties assigned on them. You already know you can pass parameters to functions. But there are also a couple of implicit parameters being passed. One is argu ments, which is useful for variable-length parameter lists. The other is this. It is called the function context, and this is always set, even when the function is not part of a class. When a function is called normally, this is the global scope (equivalent to win dow in a browser). When a function is called as a method on an object, this is referring to the object. When a function is an DOM event handler, this will be the DOM object in question.

A function can also be invoked using the new keyword. You do this when the function is a constructor, but in JavaScript the constructor is also the equivalent of the class keyword in other languages: it doesn't just do initialization tasks, it also describes what is in the object. So, inside a constructor, `this` refers to the newly created object. Here is an example:

```
function MyClass(constructorParam){
  var privateVariable = "hello";

  this.publicVariable = "world";

  var privateFunction = function(a,b){
    console.log(a + " " + b + constructorParam);
    };

  this.publicFunction = function(){
    privateFunction(
      privateVariable,
      this.publicVariable
      );
    };
  }
```

And then you use it like this:

```
var x = new MyClass("!");
x.publicFunction();
```

(This will output "hello world!" to the console.)

Notice how both `constructorParam` and `privateVariable` act like globals, but they are only visible within the public and private member functions of `MyClass`. Perfect.

The Code with Objects

So, to make an object we just need to wrap all the code in a constructor function, then put `this.` in front of everything? Here is what it looks like:

```
<!doctype html>
<html>
<head>
<meta charset="UTF-8">
<title>SSE: Basic With Sleep: OOP (doesn't work)</title>
</head>
<body>
<pre id="x">Initializing...</pre>
<script>
function SSE(url,domId){
this.es = null;
this.keepaliveSecs = 5;
this.keepaliveTimer = null;

this.gotActivity = function(){
if(this.keepaliveTimer != null)
  clearTimeout(this.keepaliveTimer);
```

```
this.keepaliveTimer = setTimeout(
  this.connect, this.keepaliveSecs * 1000);
};

this.connect = function(){
document.getElementById(domId).
  innerHTML += "\nIn connect";
if(this.es)this.es.close();
this.es = new EventSource(url);
this.es.addEventListener('message',
  function(e){this.processOneLine(e.data);},
  false);
this.gotActivity();
};

this.processOneLine = function(s){
this.gotActivity();
document.getElementById(domId).
  innerHTML += "\n" + s;
var d = JSON.parse(s);

if(d.comeBackIn10s){
  if(this.keepaliveTimer != null)
    clearTimeout(this.keepaliveTimer);
  if(this.es)this.es.close();
  setTimeout(this.connect,10*1000);
  }
};

this.connect();
}

setTimeout(function(){new SSE("basic_with_sleep.php", "x");},100);

</script>
</body>
</html>
```

Save it as *basic_with_sleep.oop1.html* and try it in the browser. Hhhmmmm…nothing happens. Firebug tells me the error is "TypeError: this.processOneLine is not a function." Oh, yes it is. Whatever does the browser think this.processOneLine = func tion(s){...} means?! It cannot be any more function-like than that. Must be a browser bug.

No. The problem is that this means something different at that line. It is the "message" *event handler* of the EventSource object. So in that event handler this is referring not to our object, but to the EventSource object.

Maybe we could do something clever by moving processOneLine on to es. Then it will be found. But then all the references to this in processOneLine will not work. No, this is the wrong tree to be barking up. There is an easier way. At the top of the constructor, make a reference to this in a private variable called self:

```
function SSE(url,domId){
var self = this;
...
```

The only other change that is needed is to change this. to self. in the "message" event handler. Nowhere else, just there.

 In fact, you could change all references to this to self in the whole class. You could even argue it is neater and tidier and therefore better.

```
this.es.addEventListener('message',
    function(e){self.processOneLine(e.data);},
    false);
```

basic_with_sleep.oop2.html does this, and if you try it you will see that this simple change got it working. Yeah! Object-oriented JavaScript to save the day. Computer scientists take a bow and then write a recursive function to pat each other on the back.

But I'm not done. Aren't you curious why the self trick worked? Aren't you curious why url and domId could be seen inside all our functions without our having to pass them around explicitly?

JavaScript Closures

The reason this works is closures. You can get a lot done with JavaScript without understanding closures, but understanding them gives you so much more power. Basically, closures mean that each time you create a function, it is given references to all the variables that were in scope at the time. I'm not going to go into any more detail; see *Secrets of the JavaScript Ninja* by John Resig and Bear Bibeault (Manning, 2012) for an in-depth explanation.

What it means for us is that when we define a variable using var in the constructor, it will be available automatically in every function we then go on to define. And, as the self example from the previous section shows, they will also be available inside functions we define inside the functions we define.[1]

---

1. Appreciating that all this stuff that is being passed around is weighing down your scripts is another reason to understand closures! The Function constructor, or the use of a function factory, are two ways to avoid closures.

It turns out we dived in, like a bull in a china shop, slapping `this.` in front of everything, when there was an easier way. Let's go back to the original code, with its four global variables and four global functions. `url` is the parameter so remove that, but just in front of the other three globals add the constructor definition, and at the end close the constructor, and call `connect()`:

```
function SSE(url){
var es = null;
var keepaliveSecs = 5;
var keepaliveTimer = null;
.
. (functions, untouched)
.
connect();
}
```

Get things started by creating an instance:

```
setTimeout(function(){
  new SSE("basic_with_sleep.php");
  }, 100);
```

If you try this out in your browser…it simply works. (See *basic_with_sleep.oop3.html* in the book's source code.) All that prefixing `this.` on either the member variables or the functions was not needed. The `self` alias was not needed.

The takeaway lesson: when you have a set of global variables, and a set of functions that operate on them, and only a single entry point from outside of those functions, wrap the whole lot in a constructor function, call the entry point from the end of the constructor, and you're done. (If you have other access points from the outside, go ahead and add public functions, using `this.XXX = function(){...}`, just for them.)

Tea for Two, and Two for Tea

To use the new constructor to run two connections, and have them update side by side, there are just a few quick changes. Add a separate DOM entry (`id="y"`) for them. Add a `domId` parameter to the constructor. And, finally, instantiate a second object (our code here uses a second timeout that starts a couple of seconds after the first one).

The full code (*basic_with_sleep.oop3.two.html*) is shown here:

```
<!doctype html>
<html>
  <head>
    <meta charset="UTF-8">
    <title>SSE: Basic With Sleep: Simple OOP and Two Instances</title>
    <style>
    pre {float:left;margin:10px;}
    </style>
  </head>
```

```
<body>
  <pre id="x">Initializing X...</pre>
  <pre id="y">Initializing Y...</pre>

  <script>
  function SSE(url,domId){
  var es = null;
  var keepaliveSecs = 5;
  var keepaliveTimer = null;

  function gotActivity(){
  if(keepaliveTimer != null)
    clearTimeout(keepaliveTimer);
  keepaliveTimer = setTimeout(
    connect, keepaliveSecs * 1000);
  }

  function connect(){
  document.getElementById(domId).
    innerHTML += "\nIn connect";
  if(es)es.close();
  gotActivity();
  es = new EventSource(url);
  es.addEventListener("message",
    function(e){processOneLine(e.data);},
    false);
  }

  function processOneLine(s){
  gotActivity();
  document.getElementById(domId).
    innerHTML += "\n" + s;
  var d = JSON.parse(s);

  if(d.comeBackIn10s){
    if(keepaliveTimer != null)
      clearTimeout(keepaliveTimer);
    if(es)es.close();
    setTimeout(connect,10*1000);
    }

  }

  connect();

  }

  setTimeout(function(){
    new SSE("basic_with_sleep.php","x");
    }, 100);
  setTimeout(function(){
    new SSE("basic_with_sleep.php","y");
```

```
    }, 2000);

  </script>
 </body>
</html>
```

 Bear in mind that modern browsers generally allow a limit of six connections to any single domain. (And those six have to include requests for images, etc., as well as Ajax requests.) So if you try adding lots of SSE objects to the preceding test page, you will only see the first six get any updates.

But, also, don't do this. Wherever possible use one SSE connection to get all the messages. Use a JSON field to identify each type of message if they are meant for different parts of your application.

There are, however, no restrictions on simultaneous connections to different servers. That is when the code in this appendix becomes useful.

PHP

PHP has been chosen as the principal language for the examples in this book, for various reasons. When combined with Apache, it allows the example code to be quite short, with very little scaffolding code needed. The syntax is straightforward and readable by anyone familiar with any mainstream programming language. And it fits the *existing infrastructure advantage* (see "Comparison with WebSockets" on page 7) of SSE very nicely, because a lot of people's existing infrastructure is already built on top of PHP.

As I said, I have tried hard to make the PHP code readable by any programmer. This appendix explains those few features where something a bit more PHP-specific was used. Explanations link directly to the related section in this appendix, at the time the feature is used.

This appendix is not intended as a general introduction to PHP. There are countless books and websites that can do that for you. The PHP online documentation (*http:// php.net/docs.php*) is an excellent starting point. If you are looking for a book in the context of dynamic websites, Robin Nixon's *Learning PHP, MySQL, JavaScript, and CSS* (O'Reilly) looks comprehensive. *Programming PHP*, by Kevin Tatroe, Peter Mac-Intyre, and Rasmus Lerdorf (O'Reilly), focuses on just the PHP language, again in the context of dynamic web pages.

Classes in PHP

Classes in PHP (as of PHP5) are closer to the classes in C++, C#, and Java than the classes you find in JavaScript, but if you have used any object-oriented language before the code used in this book should be understandable.

Each element of the class is prefixed with an access modifier: `public` or `private`. Functions are then preceded with the keyword `function`, and items without the `function` prefix are member variables. The constructor is a function that is run at the time the object is created, and is called `__construct()`. So *fxpair.seconds.php* uses encapsulation to have a number of `private` variables, a constructor to initialize those variables, and then a single public function to do something with a mix of those private variables and the function parameters it is given.

Member variables (and member functions) are accessed by prefixing with `$this->`. This is similar to JavaScript, which uses `this.` as a prefix. In other OOP languages, such as C++, the use of `this.` is considered optional (though some style guides suggest it).

For more information on OOP in PHP, please see the manual at *http://php.net/class*.

Random Functions

PHP has functions called `rand` and `mt_rand`—how to choose between them? We use `mt_rand`. The MT stands for Mersenne Twister, and gives us better-quality random numbers. (Some places also claim it is notably faster, others that `rand` and `mt_rand` are about the same speed; this appears to depend on your operating system and PHP version.)

Use `mt_srand` to set the random seed for `mt_rand`. Setting the same random seed each time allows you to get the same sequence of "random" numbers every time. This is wonderful for repeatable testing. If you want different random numbers each time, there is no particular need to call `mt_srand` because PHP will initialize the seed for you (based on the current server clock).

Superglobals

PHP has some *super*globals, which are available in all functions, and give you ready-parsed information about the request, as well about the machine environment. They are all associative arrays. `$_GET` is the HTTP GET data, `$_POST` is the HTTP POST data, and `$_COOKIES` is…well, you guessed it. `$_SERVER` will tell you other information about the request, while `$_ENV` will tell you about the machine you are running on. `$GLOBALS` gives access to user-defined global variables.

There is also `$_REQUEST`, which is a combination of all of `$_GET`, `$_POST`, and `$_COOKIES`. Be aware that using `$_REQUEST` is usually discouraged, because there are security implications of cookie data overriding your form data. You should use `$_REQUEST`—and *only* use `$_REQUEST`—when the variable you are interested in could validly have come from any of GET, POST, or cookie data.

However, note that since PHP 5.3, the default *php.ini* file will exclude cookie data from `$_REQUEST`. See *http://php.net/request_order*. So, you now have to set `request_order` to "CGP" if you explicitly want to allow cookies to be included in `$_REQUEST`. By putting "C" first, POST gets priority over GET, which gets priority over cookie data.

Date Handling

PHP has some powerful functions for dealing with times and dates. `time` returns the time in seconds since 1970; we have seen it before. Another couple we have seen before are `date()` and `gmdate()`, which turn Unix time into a string for local and GMT time zones, respectively. They come with more format options than you can shake a stick at —take a look at *http://php.net/date*.

If I had to name a single PHP function I miss more than any other when using other languages, it is `strtotime()`. This takes a date in string form and returns it in Unix time (seconds since January 1, 1970). Of course it deals with standard timestamp formats, such as "2013-12-25 13:25:50," as well as dealing with the month in words, e.g., "25th December 2013." But it gets better! You can also give date offsets, so you can write `strtotime("+1 day")` to get the timestamp for 24 hours from now. You can write "last day of February." And you can write "next month," "last Thursday," etc.

By default, the calculations are relative to the current time. But by specifying the second parameter you can have it relative to any other time. And that second parameter could be using `strtotime` too! Here is an example that finds the last Friday before Christmas in the year 2001:

```
$friday = strtotime("last Friday",
    strtotime("2001-12-25"));
echo date("Y-m-d",$friday);
//2001-12-21
```

Passwords

User passwords should obviously not be stored in a database as plain text. Though better than nothing, encryption is also usually a bad idea—if the key is stolen, all the passwords can be recovered. Instead of encryption you should be *hashing* your passwords. Hashing is a one-way process: it takes the plain-text password, and applies a number of mathematical operations to it to give some random-looking string. You cannot reverse the operation, and there is no key to be stolen. But given the same plain-text password, you will always get the same hashed password out of the algorithm.

However, with rogues and rogue governments building faster and faster computers to hack you, your grandfather's password hashing algorithms are no longer good enough. It used to be that `md5()` was enough, and if you used `salt` with it you could hold your head high in the nerdiest of company. But no longer.

As of PHP 5.5.0 the security best practice is to use `password_hash()` to make your passwords, and `password_verify()` to validate them. If you are using an earlier version

of PHP, add the following code to the top of your script[1] (the if(!defined(...))
{...} wrapper simply means this block will be ignored when the script is run on PHP
5.5 or later):

```
if (!defined("PASSWORD_DEFAULT")) {
function password_hash($password){
$salt = str_replace("+", ".", base64_encode(sha1(time(),true)));
$salt = substr($salt, 0, 22); //We want exactly 22 characters
if(PHP_VERSION_ID<50307)return crypt($password, '$2a$10$'.$salt);
else return crypt($password, '$2y$10$'.$salt);
}

function password_verify($password, $hash) {
return crypt($password,$hash) === $hash;
}

}   //End of if (!defined('PASSWORD_DEFAULT'))
```

PHP 5.3.7 introduced a new, better hashing algorithm. The preceding code uses that
when available; otherwise, it uses the previous best choice. The 10 in '$2y$10$' is a
measure of how slow to be. In the weird world of password hashing, slow is good; 10 is
the default as of PHP 5.5. It means password hashing might take a significant fraction
of a CPU second. Read the PHP manual's descriptions of these functions if you want to
tweak these parameters. To be future-proof, use a VARCHAR(255) field for storing password hashes in an SQL database, though currently they will always be exactly 60 characters long.

Falling Asleep

There are two easily confused functions in PHP: sleep() and usleep(). The former
takes an integer, the number of seconds to sleep. The latter also takes an integer, but as
the number of microseconds to sleep. So, for example, sleep(2) and us
leep(2000000) are identical; they both put the script to sleep for two seconds. However,
if you want to sleep for 0.25 seconds, or 1.5 seconds, your only choice is to use usleep
(usleep(250000) and usleep(1500000), respectively).

This is a good time to mention max_execution_time (a configuration setting) and
set_time_limit() (a function to allow resetting the max_execution_time). The special
value of zero means "run forever," and that is the default when you run scripts from the
command line. However, through a web browser, the default is 30 seconds; with Linux/
Mac, that is 30 seconds of CPU time, but with Windows it is measured as wall-clock
time. For a streaming server, that 30 seconds will come quite quickly; you might not
even notice unless you look at your browser console, but your SSE script will end up

---

1. For a more comprehensive version of the PHP 5.5 functions, see *https://github.com/ircmaxell/pass
word_compat*.

reconnecting to the backend every 30 seconds. (Unless doing something compute-intensive, over on Linux you won't notice it for tens of minutes or even hours.)

The fix is simple—at the very top of your script add this line:

```
set_time_limit(0);
```

Index

Symbols

? (question mark), 49
@ (at sign), 21

A

about:config Mozilla feature, 57
access control, 146–148
Access-Control-Allow-Credentials, 152
Access-Control-Allow-Headers, 149
Access-Control-Allow-Origin, 145, 151
ActiveXObject, 71
Ajax, 4, 91
    readyState, 105
Allow header, 148
Apache servers
    authorization with, 137–139
    data compression and, 82
application example, 6
    (see also production-quality applications)
    about, 6
    adding history store, 51–55
    allowing for passage of time, 44
    backend, 20–27, 30–33
    controlling randomness, 42–44
    frontend, 15–19, 35
    grafting long-poll onto, 94–103
    grafting XHR/iframe onto, 113–118
    optimization possibilities, 56

persistent storage, 55–57
problem domain, 29–30
putting it together, 160–166
realistic, repeatable, random data, 36–39
reducing size of data, 57
refactoring JavaScript, 49–51
refactoring PHP script, 48
structuring data, 47–48
timestamps, 39–42
usage summary, 120
at sign (@), 21
authentication, multiple choices, 141–142
authorization
    Access-Control-Allow-Origin, 145
    with Apache, 137–139
    browsers and CORS, 150
    constructors and credentials, 151–152
    cookies, 136–137
    CORS and, 143–145, 153–157
    fine access control, 146–148
    HTTP HEAD, 148
    HTTP OPTIONS, 148
    HTTP POST with SSE, 139–141
    multiple authentication choices, 141–142
    putting example together, 160–166

B

backend
    allowing for passage of time, 44

We'd like to hear your suggestions for improving our indexes. Send email to index@oreilly.com.

About the Author

Darren Cook has more than 20 years of experience as a software developer and technical director, working on everything from financial trading systems, through data visualization tools, through PR websites for some of the world's largest brands, all the way to arcade games. He is skilled in a wide range of computer languages, including JavaScript, PHP, and C++. He has developed systems around HTTP streaming web services (such as Twitter), written many low-level direct socket server/client protocols in numerous applications, and built applications with both SSE and WebSockets.

Colophon

The animal on the cover of *Data Push Apps with HTML5 SSE* is a short-beaked echidna (*Tachyglossus aculeatus*). The four species of echidnas, along with the platypus, are the only mammals who lay eggs instead of giving birth to live young. The short-beaked echidna is found in forested areas of Australia (where it is the most widespread native mammal) and parts of New Guinea.

Short-beaked echidnas are 12–18 inches long, with brown fur and cream-colored spines (made of keratin) on their back. True to their name, their snouts are about 3 inches long, shorter than other echidna species. The leathery snout serves multiple purposes: its wedge shape is optimized to explore insect mounds, it has electroreceptors that help detect nearby prey, and its labyrinth-like bone structure is believed to help condense exhaled water vapor and cool the animal down (since echidnas do not have sweat glands).

Echidnas are sometimes called spiny anteaters, though this term has fallen out of use since they are not actually related to true anteaters. Their diet is indeed made up of insects, however—mostly ants and termites, which they catch by digging into the insects' nests and capturing prey with their long sticky tongues. Echidnas are expert diggers, thanks to their specialized claws and strong short limbs. Apart from hunting prey, they also dig as a defense mechanism; if threatened, they will burrow very quickly into the ground and roll into a ball, leaving only their sharp spines exposed. They are also capable swimmers, which they do with only their nose above water, like a snorkel.

The short-beaked echidna appears on the reverse side of Australia's 5-cent coin, and has even made it into videogames, as the character Knuckles in the classic *Sonic the Hedgehog* series.

The cover image is from Wood's *Animate Creation*. The cover fonts are URW Typewriter and Guardian Sans. The text font is Adobe Minion Pro; the heading font is Adobe Myriad Condensed; and the code font is Dalton Maag's Ubuntu Mono.

Have it your way.

O'Reilly eBooks

- Lifetime access to the book when you buy through oreilly.com
- Provided in up to four DRM-free file formats, for use on the devices of your choice: PDF, .epub, Kindle-compatible .mobi, and Android .apk
- Fully searchable, with copy-and-paste and print functionality
- Alerts when files are updated with corrections and additions

oreilly.com/ebooks/

Safari Books Online

- Access the contents and quickly search over 7000 books on technology, business, and certification guides
- Learn from expert video tutorials, and explore thousands of hours of video on technology and design topics
- Download whole books or chapters in PDF format, at no extra cost, to print or read on the go
- Get early access to books as they're being written
- Interact directly with authors of upcoming books
- Save up to 35% on O'Reilly print books

See the complete Safari Library at safari.oreilly.com

Get even more for your money.

Join the O'Reilly Community, and register the O'Reilly books you own. It's free, and you'll get:

- $4.99 ebook upgrade offer
- 40% upgrade offer on O'Reilly print books
- Membership discounts on books and events
- Free lifetime updates to ebooks and videos
- Multiple ebook formats, DRM FREE
- Participation in the O'Reilly community
- Newsletters
- Account management
- 100% Satisfaction Guarantee

Signing up is easy:

1. **Go to: oreilly.com/go/register**
2. **Create an O'Reilly login.**
3. **Provide your address.**
4. **Register your books.**

Note: English-language books only

To order books online:
oreilly.com/store

For questions about products or an order:
orders@oreilly.com

To sign up to get topic-specific email announcements and/or news about upcoming books, conferences, special offers, and new technologies:
elists@oreilly.com

For technical questions about book content:
booktech@oreilly.com

To submit new book proposals to our editors:
proposals@oreilly.com

O'Reilly books are available in multiple DRM-free ebook formats. For more information:
oreilly.com/ebooks

Spreading the knowledge of innovators　　　　oreilly.com

Ingram Content Group UK Ltd.
Milton Keynes UK
UKHW052114210623
423829UK00010B/445